YOU'D BE SO NICE TO COME HOME TO

The Letters of
Paul "Buddy" Frees
&
Annelle Frees

Edited by

Ben Ohmart

BearManor Media
Albany, Georgia

Published in the USA by:
BearManor Media
PO Box 1129
Duncan, OK 73534-1129
www.BearManorMedia.com

ISBN 1-59393-646-X
ISBN-13: 978-1-59393-646-4

Printed in the United States.

Design and Layout by Allan T. Duffin.

Dedication

For June Lewis and Family

Thank you for your wonderful generosity

Table of Contents

Editor's Note

This book is meant to be a supplement to my biography, *Welcome, Foolish Mortals: The Life and Voices of Paul Frees,* and probably won't make much sense to anyone who hasn't read that book. Paul was arguably the greatest voice actor who ever lived, born into a time when the celebrity voice had not taken over. His vast skill of accents and comedy prevailed over many a cartoon, film, trailer, radio show, and TV program.

My book came out in 2004. Since then, I've been fortunate enough to have lucked into further information about Paul, most notably in the form of the "missing wives." The most significant being letters to and from Paul's first wife, Annelle, during their heartbreaking years of separation during World War II. While the horrors of the war are only hinted at, we might say that on the plus side, because of the war, there's more of a permanent record of Paul's early years, before he became a showbiz professional, than we otherwise would have had.

These letters have been kept for nearly 70 years by Annelle's sister, June Lewis and her family, and without June, who found me, there would be no book.

I haven't been much of an editor, since there isn't much to add to what's here. There are some cryptic lines in what you're about to read, like September 21, 1944's mention of "glad you had the peanuts poisoned." I can't even guess what that means. So rather than edit out the unexplained and the highly repetitive ("Kiss Olivia [June Lewis] for me"), I've included every word Annelle Frees wrote for the sake of completeness and to retain the flavor of a very lonely woman in an era of war and hope. (These letters were typed just as written, including underlines, spacings, dashes, etc.)

Ironically, her letters end just as the war ends, and as Annelle is about to go into the hospital. "Annelle had some difficult female problems," states June, "and, we think, was at one time pregnant. She lost the baby and continued to have the problems, so the doctor believed she needed surgery. She went through the operation and was almost ready to come home, but developed peritonitis [an inflammation of the membrane which lines the inside of the abdomen and all of the internal organs] and died.

"From some of Paul's letters, it seems the hospital did not recommend her being moved to another hospital. Her death was not expected from what I gathered, and from what mother told us."

Paul Frees said later that the death of his first wife changed his life—that he had lost the love of his life. Who knows how Paul's personal history might have changed had poor lovely young Annelle lived.

"I asked my brother if our Dad showed any anger when Paul brought Annelle's body back for burial," says June. "He said he did not. In fact, he said Paul spent the night at the house and he and Dad sat out on the porch that night and talked.

"He said Buddy really loved mother's fried chicken and iced tea! Almost sounds like a true Southerner, hum? Even though I was very young, and do not actually remember anything about Annelle, I want to share with others what a wonderful, loving wife, sister and daughter she was.

"This was not that long after the Depression, and during the war, and things were very hard to come by. Outside of the fact that my family was, like most everyone else, poor (in material things, but rich in love), Annelle was always trying to get things, not just for the immediate family, but for some of the extended family. Truly, she was a beautiful person inside and out.

"I checked with David, my brother, to make sure I had the story correct about how Annelle and Paul met. He is better about remembering things mother shared with us than I am. Annelle was working at Ft. Rucker, Alabama, where Paul was stationed. One day Paul went into this place where she was working, saw her, and asked someone in there about her. The person knew a few things about her; she was, at the time, living with mother's father and two unmarried sisters in Slocomb, Alabama, which was nearer to Rucker. One of the aunt's names was Norma, which the person told Paul about and about her living with them. The next time he went in there he walked over to Annelle's desk and showed her he had handwritten 'Ann,' and told her he knew something about her. She questioned him as to what he meant and he said, 'I know your name is

Audrey Annelle, you live in Slocomb with your Aunt Norma.' From that grew the relationship and it was not too much longer after they were married. I guess you could say it was one of those 'love at first sight's."

§

Miss Audrey McLeod
Box 2
Slocomb, Alabama

SERVICE COMPANY, 137th INFANTRY
35th DIVISION

June I

Dear Audrey:

Well, here I am writing you as I
promised I would —— I can't begin to tell
you what a really delightful time I had
in your town — And I do think the people
I met there, were the nicest I have ever
had the good fortune of meeting.! ——

I have been terribly busy here at
camp, as it is the end of the month, and all
regimental business must be terminated &
settled before the new month begins ——

I will be unable to see you on Thur.
as I must remain in camp & do company duty.
However, I want to take this written opportunity
to wish you happiness, success, and a bright
future on this, the occasion of your graduation —
I'm sure, that now that you've reached
(paper conservation - over)

Buddy's Letters
to Audrey (Annelle)

June 1, 1943
[Service Company, 137th Infantry, 35 Division stationery]

Dear Audrey:

Well, here I am writing you as I promised I would—I can't begin to tell you what a really delightful time I had in your town—And I do think the people I met there, were the nicest I have ever had the good fortune of meeting!!

I have been terribly busy here at camp, as it is the end of the month, and all regimental business must be terminated & settled before the new month begins.

I will be unable to see you on Thur. as I must remain in camp & do company duty. However, I want to take this written opportunity to wish you happiness, success, and a bright maturity, that you will find the world a place of wondrous treasures—But remember, to partake of the beauties, & pleasures you must also learn to endure the hardships & trials of our peculiar world-------.

(Please forgive the above philosophizing, it's just one of my peculiarities.)

No kidding, Audrey, I do wish you the best & wish I could get there to say so in person, however, duty to God & Country before __?..?...? *[sic]*

Well, guess I had better close now, as I must get my work completed before night falls----.

Incidentally, I'll be unable to make it Sunday, either----------.

> *Write soon*
> *Buddy*

P.S. Give my best wishes to Aunt Les & Norma & Grandpop & all the rest. *B.*

June 6, 1943
[Postcard by way of USO mail]

Surprise! (Look at postmark.)

Yes, I'm in Memphis, Tenn. & will be in Arkansas in a few hours, where I am going to see a friend----------

I'll be back next week & get in touch with you then!! OK?

> Buddy

§

June 21 or July 8, 1943
[United States Army stationery]

Dear Audrey:

Thank you for the letter, & I'm sorry I was unable to answer it sooner than I have, however, we are temporarily incapacitated & unable to do many of the things I would like to.

I hope you weren't too disappointed last Wednesday, but really we just couldn't make it to the U.S.O. No, I didn't feel angry about anything last week & I didn't make it back (to you) because I couldn't find a place to rest------------.

I have disregarded your letter as you requested on the post-card, but nonetheless, it was a very interesting Billet-Doux, I must say.

Well, I think I had better close now as we must go about some very urgent business------------------write soon.

> As ever---
> Buddy

§

June 29, 1943

Audrey:

Thank you for the lovely letter. I regret terribly that I have been unable to meet you at any occasion of the past couple of weeks, but I have been in the hospital, and am still in it!----I didn't deem it necessary to tell you before, but now that I am sure to be released in another day or two, it shouldn't harm to tell you----Aren't I the inflated ego to think that by not telling you I had spared you what concern you may have had for me--------In so far as headaches is concerned I have quite a head on my shoulders—7 3/8 to be exact------

How long have you been working at the hat shop? Is it interesting and profitable?---

I suppose you can hardly suppress the desire to know what my ailment is?

Well, it was thought to be a form of ulcer or something. However it has proven to be nothing more than a gastric hyper acidity and few other things of reasonably little consequence.

Please don't try to come & see me, because it is not bad, really---& besides, I am being held almost incommunicado---

Well, guess I better close now, so write me a nice big letter, huh?

Buddy

§

July 8, 1943
[Typed on United States Army stationery]

Thursday
Dear Audrey:

Thank you for the letter. I am now officially released from the hospital, and I hope I never see the place again..... I feel as good as new however and I am grateful for the attention and treatment I received there......

I will try to get in touch with you as soon as I can, but I am so busy I don't know when it will be.....I will try to get in this Saturday or Sunday if possible... OK??

So you are back at the five and ten? Well, big oaks from little acorns grow and who knows but maybe someday you may be the boss in the place?

Keep trying anyway.....

I was very glad to hear of Mary's connubial bliss and if you correspond with her I wish you would convey my best wishes to her and her hubby...

How are Nadine and John? and Aunt Les and Norma?.......Perhaps you can answer those in person if I get in this weekend.....

Yes, it has been terribly hot here and especially in the Hospital, I doubt if I ever got any sleep there because of the heat that was there...

But it seems to be just as bad in the barracks.

Oh well, such are the trials and tribulations of a soldier in the Service of his country, EH?

I must close now (altho I would like to continue), it seems I have a bit of work I must do before my boss catches up with me, and the Col. just issued an ultimatum that my office WILL be clean, so I will spend the next few hours discarding accumulated papers and records and such which are now passé....

Well, hope to see you this Saturday, I'll call your house, so leave word where you are if you are working or out somewhere...

Buddy

§

Undated, but thought to be August 20, 1943.
[Written on "American Red Cross" stationery]

Sun.

Dear Audrey:

Thank you for your letter. I am still in the hospital, but I shall be out shortly, (I hope).

Where are you working now that you've left the hat shop? Are you but a "lady of leisure"?

It has been so darned uncomfortable here because of the heat, I can't wait to get out again. / ------------------

How are all your girl friends back in Slocomb? or don't you get back there at all? ------

I will try to come & see you the first opportunity I get after getting out ---- o.k.?

Have you been having fun? From your last letter, you sound as if you "don't get around much anymore"!! True? -----------

Well, I must close now & go back to bed as it is 8:45 pm. & the lights go out at 9:00 so ------------------------- Write soon.

Buddy

§

November 22, 1943

Sun.

My Dearest wife:

To date I have received 4 of your letters and really honey, I don't think you could be any more unhappy than I am------I do miss you so much!!---I am in Lebanon (a small town nearby) to close our canteen account until next week---------. I have been so busy, that I haven't even had a chance to eat a good meal for 2 days--(now, don't worry, baby, I'm o.k.)—. We go on our problem tomorrow & so I guess it will mean no rest for another 4 days------.

Really, baby, I think I'd give up my right arm to have been with you for this week-end—but, such is the fortunes of war-------.

From the way things look honey, I don't think there is any sense in your coming here to stay, because Nashville is a place I'll never be able to go to—& this town Lebanon has a population of 5,000 & I can't even get a pass to come here, because I am working every week-end-------

Had a letter from my Mom & Mannie is out of the Army-----At present he is visiting Rose in Chicago & then he will proceed to California---(Forgive me for rushing honey, but I just stole these few minutes to write to you & must now return)-----------

Well, dearest, please don't feel too badly & don't be discouraged ----- our day is yet to come!! Yes? Well, be good, God Bless you. Remember, I love you—

    Your loving husband,
    Buddy

§

November 24, 1943

Thurs.

My Dearest:

Thank you for your letter, Baby. It made me so happy to hear from you!! (excuse the handwriting but I'm writing on my knee, it's the only place around here to write on!) We got here yesterday afternoon & set up our tent–(Slusky & I are bunking together) What a place, it is all wilderness & pretty cold, but I think I'll make it alright—

The trip was pretty tiresome, being pushed in the back end of a truck for 3 days wasn't any fun, but now that we are here, all I've got to worry about is 60 some days of living in the forest—

We haven't been out of our clothes yet, & the way it looks, we will stay in them for the rest of maneuvers!

Oh well, such is life—Honey, please don't forget to write, because your letters are the only happy thing about this whole affair—I miss you so much, sweet, and am just waiting for the day when we can be together again!!-----

Honey, I know it was hard for you to leave me & it hurt me just as much to think of being here, away from you, but try & keep your chin up, & this will all be over before we realize it ----

(While I'm writing, Slusky is tearing a tree apart to put on the fire, it is our only means of keeping warm until we go to sleep-----.)

Well, dearest, I'm afraid I must close now, as I have some work to do before supper—so, write soon. Give my love to Mother, dad, & the kids—and remember, I love you,

> *your loving husband,*
> *Buddy*

§

November 26, 1943

Wed.

My Beloved Wife:

Thank you for your letters, just received the ones you wrote Sat. & Sun.

Honey, I have written you 3 times so far, & yet you say you haven't gotten one (a letter) as yet—

By this time, you must surely have them—(I am writing this letter on the back of a small trench shovel, so please forgive.)

Honey, if I don't write to you as often as I should like to, it is merely because we are so busy that it is impossible—Let me explain the circumstances—you see, for 4 days (Mon. thru Thurs.) we are tactical which means no light of any kind at night & we are on the move & working all day!! During those 4 days, I don't do Special Service work at all, but instead I am on guard duty—and believe me, it is rough!!—For a few hours during the day it is fairly warm but then...it starts getting cold & - ice cold! We all are suffering from frost bite here & there is no way of getting even slightly warm because fires aren't permitted— Speaking of free time. None of us have had a shave in a week or a bath, or even washed!!—Even if we had time, there isn't any water so what the hell—Toujours gai!! Toujours gai!! We are having a few free minutes now, while we wait for trucks to take us to the front lines again. (Pardon the stationary, but it is some I kept in my pocket, hoping for a few free moments like this—)

Honey Baby, I miss you, & all I can think about is when we'll be together again.

No kidding, baby, I'll dream about you the first chance I get to sleep for awhile!

You see, the weekends are the only time we get to sleep, & that's when I have to do Special Service work!! So between being on guard all week, I have to work on weekend rest periods also!!—Oh well, maybe it will make the time go faster!!—

Then we can be together again!!—

Well, darling, I must go now, so write soon. Give my love to your family for me—& give all my love & my kisses to you—

I love you darling—

Your loving husband,

Buddy

P.S. How about writing me some news, what you're doing, what goes on in Dothan, etc.?

§

November 26, 1943

Thurs.

(Thanksgiving)

My Dearest Wife:

Just read your letter of Monday—Thank you so much my darling for writing so consistently, honest, your letters & the thought that we will be together again, is the only thing that keeps me going—Honey, the reason you may not have received any of my letters as yet may be because they don't let the letters out until the end of the week------. Dearest, I don't see how you can come to Nashville & see me because we have never been into Nashville yet & won't even be there—as I explained in one of my letters, dearest, we work all week & all weekend (that is, I do, anyway).

Honey, I do miss you so much—you know I love you, darling, and every minute away from you makes me realize that I can't go anywhere without you----.

Just think, darling, how wonderful it will be when we finally do get re-united!

We'll certainly raise a little hell, won't we darling? Gee honey, I'm so darn lonesome for you I could cry (even as tough & rugged as I am!).

Don't you worry, baby, as soon as we get off of this "Devil's Tour," we'll be together & I defy hell an' highwater to tear us apart. But, for the present we can do nothing but hope & pray for our future!! Yes?

Right now we are in a "crummy" area we just moved into at 3:00 a.m. & everyone is dog tired, but we're all going to shave & wash (for the first time in a week)—We'll have hot water because we heat it in our helmets over a fire!!—

No conveniences out here, you know-----.

Well, my love, I guess I better close now, (I hate to stop writing, because while I write to you, it is as tho I am there with you). Incidentally, dearest, I read your last letter 8 times which is less than I usually read your letters, but before the day is over, I imagine I shall have kept up my record of at least 10 times each---- Well, love, write me soon, I love you with all my heart. Happy Thanksgiving. (Eat some turkey for me!!)

> *Your loving husband,*
> *Buddy*

§

November 28, 1943
[Written on "Tennessee Maneuvers 'Somewhere in Tennessee'" stationery]

Sat.

My Dearest:

Just got your Tuesday letter. It was so sweet honey, and means so much to me----.

I'm so sorry I haven't written the past 4 days darling, but I have been so busy, I didn't have time—Right now I'm taking an hour off waiting for Lt. Brown to come back from Lebanon with more canteen supplies—(We sold all we had bought this afternoon.)

Damnit, honey, right now I'm so mad I could massacre someone!!—That darn Lt. Brown is so hairbrain he doesn't know if he is coming or going!!----

He runs around like a chicken without a head, the jerk comes on the week-ends & gets me in the wee hours of the morning & doesn't even give me a chance to lace my shoes or anything!!—Thank goodness I don't see him during the week because I'm on guard, so that proves to be a consolation----

Honest, darling, I haven't had an opportunity to even wash the past few days!! (I did wash & shower since I wrote you last!)—I think that I will be put on detached service for the next week only, so that I can write a broadcast for 2nd Army—it is a half hour show that goes coast-to-coast & will transmit from a Nashville station—I'll have to do so much work on it as I did on the one I did from Rucker!

Oh well, if I finish it o.k. & if I don't well, let them sue me----.

God, honey, this darn place is a madhouse!! And... I'm going mad with them!!—(Don't worry honey, it isn't really bad, I'm just lost right now & I'll feel better in a little while----.)

If only I could be with you for a little while, honey, I know I'd feel better, but-----

I haven't had a pass yet, & it looks like I won't get one either, for the rest of maneuvers.

They say we all will get our furlos right after maneuvers, so we'll be together then, anyway.

Dearest, I will try to get to a phone on Christmas to call you, but I can't be sure—Tell me where & what time you'll be Christmas so I'll know where to call—

Darling, thank Doris & Annette for their letters & tell them I just haven't the time or I would write to them----.

I promise I will the first chance I get!--------------.

Honey, you never mention how the operation on that mole on your nose turned out? Did it hurt you? I do hope not & I hope you are all well by now!-----. Baby, you say you are too weak to write! What is the matter, darling? Is it your cold? Or is it something else?

Please, honey, you must take care of yourself & get well for me-----.

Remember, dearest, I love you. & I want you to be well & happy 'till I get back-----.

Well sweet, I must close now & get back to work. I'll write again as soon as I possibly can, so please don't worry about me, baby.-----------------------.

Give my love to the family.

Your loving husband,

Buddy

§

Possibly December 1, 1943
[Written on USO stationery]

My Darling:

Thank you for the letter (two came today)—But, honey, I'm sorry you are ill—now baby, if you have the "flu" you mustn't exert yourself any—rest, and warmth will cure you, so please, sweet, don't take any chances—. After all baby, if you should get sick, I can't be there to comfort you—(great help I'd be—).

At present, I am in Lebanon, turning in funds for the canteen, & the Lt. is giving us some off time to look around a bit before we return to the bivouac area------.

(Funny, a soldier was sitting here in the writing room and whistling "Pistol Packin' Mama," and I felt like telling him to stop because I'm writing to my wife & she doesn't like that song!!

Crazy that, isn't it?)

Honest, dearest, nothing makes sense to me since your *[sic]* not here with me—I love you so much, baby. God, I wish I were there so I could tell you in person—(Dearest, wish hard now, close your eyes & I'm there with you!!—Am I?)

I'm doing it now, I can almost reach out & feel you there—Honey—I just kissed you--------.

Oh nuts!!------.

Honey, I know how much our being together Christmas means to you, & it means a lot to me too, but, really, there isn't any way at all we could possibly be together—I know, baby, I hate to think that we have to wait almost 3 more months before we can see each other, but, for the present, that's the way it looks----------.

Darling, please don't worry about me, because I'll be o.k.—I can take anything they give as long as I have you to think about-------.

Well, my beloved, I must close now, so take care of yourself, please get well, I love you, your,

Buddy

§

December 5, 1943
[Written on United States Army stationery]

Tues.

My Dearest:

Just a note to let you know I am still in camp and although I'm not working hard, I am rather tired & very lonesome for you!

I may have to take a canteen to the field this warm, sultry afternoon and I am waiting for the "Boss" to give me instructions—I didn't see a letter from you as yet, but that is probably due to the fact that the mail will be delivered from the mail dept., which is out in the field.

I do hope everything is well with you & that you don't feel badly—I should be able to get into town this week-end & then we'll have a [unreadable] together—o.k. Honey?—I haven't heard from the Major in Maryland as yet, but that is probably due to the mail situation—I must admit, however, I am not anticipating anything too much to our favor, so don't lets build our hopes too high!------------

Well, my darling, I must close now, as the "Boss" just came in!--------

Please think of me---I do of you-------Your loving husband

    Buddy

§

Undated
[Stationery at top reads: Tennessee Maneuvers "Somewhere in Tennessee"]

Mon.

Huwo Darling:

Had another letter from you today!!-----(The brightest thing in my present existence!) It will be dark in another half hour or so & then we will probably move before the enemy catches up to us.

About the radio show I was going to do, I won't be doing it, (yippee), mainly because I wasn't given any time & secondly because I can't be released from the company for the week it would take----.

I'm not sad however, because all it was as far as I was concerned was another headache!!

Gosh honey, I think all I've accomplished today is thinking of you, & that isn't work---it's a pleasure!

Really, that is all I could think of my darling—YOU!!

I love you darling—And, here is the kiss for you--- [Arrow points to empty box. Another small arrow points from this sentence to box.] This space reserved for a kiss to my darling wife.

Damnit but this has been a miserable day!

Mud, mud & more mud right up to our ankles. Right now we are located on the near top of a large hill & the trucks can't get up here, because the mud is so slippery----------.

Slusky just came in (we have our tent in a wooded area & we built a little living room in front of the tent flap----. Our floor rug is a boggy mud hole, but we call it home)

Incidentally, dearest, Slus & I & just about everyone here have grown mustaches & some have beards. The reason is obvious------.

I had a very shaggy looking mustache & this morning Lt. Kain saw me & he & two other of the boys caught me & trimmed it up---. I do believe it looks better (if I can ever look good to begin with!!) Honey, baby, I'm so sorry your [sic] not feeling too well--------.

I hope your [sic] better by now, dearest. Darling, I have a confession to make; I is a bad boy—Oh! yes I is!!

When I went into Lebanon yesterday to check in the canteen, I took about fifteen minutes off & happened to run into a beautiful blonde. She really was a honey, blue eyes, blond & so damn sweet. I really fell in love with her—now, I intended being true to you, but this girl smiled at me & I couldn't resist!!----Are you jealous, honey?—You needn't be, she was only 18 months old—honest, darling, she was the sweetest baby you've ever seen!!--------She had a tiny little ring on her finger and the brightest smile—I guess I was attracted to her because she was about the cleanest thing I've seen hereabouts.

Nuts, here I am talking about babies!!----------------It's all your fault, you just make me think about anything sweet, good, kind, pure, lovable, darling, choice, etc., etc.----- (Whoops!! just now a whole flock of little pigs came oinking by—they frequently pass thru foraging for food)-------

Well dearest, it is getting a bit too dark now, so I better close & send this---

Remember, sweetheart, I love you, only you--------- your
Buddy

§

December 11, 1943

Fri.

My Dearest:

I am rushing this note, as I haven't but a moment or two----

I got 3 of your letters today and, honey, I am so happy you are all better-----.

Darling, let me remind you, if you don't get a letter when you should from me, it is because I am so busy, or in a place where I can't write—This week has been a hectic affair—We keep moving constantly & what's more it has rained all week & the mud is actually up to our knees!!–No kidding honey, it is so bad, we are sleeping half in it because there isn't a dry spot anywhere!!—Darling, you mustn't worry about me, because honest, I haven't been sick a minute!!------------. I feel fine, & my spirits are high even if it is cold & muddy!!—Really, darling, I don't mind anything we do here one tenth as much as I feel about being away from you!!—(I hope you can read this letter, I'm writing about 200 per.)

Honey, I appreciate your wanting to send me a ham or something, but I don't think it advisable because I wouldn't have any place to keep it—Thank your folks for it too, but at present I'll do without it----------.

Honey, let me say again, please don't worry too much because I'll be alright—Just keep your letters coming—(you have no idea what a moral uplift they are!!)

Well, dearest, I have to close now, so be good, love me & remember darling, I think of you every minute because I love you so much—so-oo-oo much that is impossible to make a pencil tell you-----------

I love you darling—
Buddy
P.S. I love you-----

§

December 21, 1943
[Stationery at top reads: Tennessee Maneuvers "Somewhere in Tennessee"]

Fri.

My Dearest:

Here it is Fr. and the first opportunity I have to write in a week!-------. I haven't had a letter from you for 6 days now, but I imagine they just can't get the mail thru to us because we are moving constantly-----at present I am sitting cross-legged by a tiny fire that I just built—(we just moved in here 5 minutes ago). This would be a pretty location ordinarily but under the present circumstances...)

Honey, I am really worried about not hearing from you, & if it is because you haven't written, please don't wait any longer------Honey, if you are sick & just don't want me to know, please don't hide it from me because you know your [sic] my wife & I love you darling & if anything is wrong I do want to know!------. I saw "Chuddles" today for a couple of minutes & he seems comparatively well------.

Hold it honey, here is "Chuddles," he just walked up & wanted to know if everything's o.k. I'll let him say hello--------. [Written in different handwriting] Hi sugar, long time, no see. Buddy tells me that you're becoming quite the aristocrat what with driving that Buick around and all. But this nonsense about your being ill—how do you expect us to be on our toes when we're worrying about you? Be good, we'll be seeing you—Chuddles

[Paul's writing] See, that was he!!—he says he's getting "bivouakky." We all are for that matter!!—

We have been having zero weather here but as yet it hasn't snowed-----. Br-r-r—it really is cold & all we have for cover are 4 blankets—2 under & two over—

Remember all the blankets we used to pile on us?------ah, how cozy!!----- Honey, would it be trite to say I love you? I do darling & it seems no matter how many times I say it, it is never enuf!-----(this is 30 minutes later.) Had to wander off for a little while & take care of a detail----

Well, honey, it won't be long now, will it? We're almost halfway thru & then....... Gad, it is almost too good to believe!!—

Baby, pardon the handwriting but I have written this letter in about 10 different positions---------

I heard a rumor that there will not be passes of any kind for Christmas, so if you don't get a phone call, you'll know the reason why-----------.

Well, my darling, I must close, I have, as usual, a mess of work to do & no time to do it—So, goodnite my honey. God Bless you. I love you & please write soon—

Your loving husband,
Buddy

§

December 21, 1943
[Written on USO stationery]

Sun.

My Dearest Wife:

Finally!! After 8 days of waiting for a letter from you, I have received 3 at one time!-----.

How do you like your new home, darling? I do hope it is nice & warm & comfortable—I often wonder what it will be like to sleep in a bed again!

It won't be long now, my sweet, in one month we'll be out of this miserable situation and without any doubt it will be to a place considerably nicer!!-------.

We haven't heard as yet where we go or whether we get our "furlos" immediately thereafter, but it is quite a comforting thought that rest & comfort are close at hand!—

It is becoming quite cold out here & at times unbearable but if the other boys can take it and not complain, rest assured I'll not be the first!----

Honey, your letters are so sweet & I just wish that I were capable of telling you how I feel but I'm afraid that will have to wait until we are together because I don't think I could even express in writing the fullness that my heart has for you-------.

I love you, my dearest, and if that will not suffice, multiply that by a billion & you have a comparative equivalent of how much I do!!—

Lt. Brown started to tell me of the work I must do Christmas day & I told him not to count on me at noon & come hell or highwater I'll be at a 'phone a calling you as I promised I would----------.

Oh honey, you can't imagine how lonely I am for you!!----------------.

I don't know, it seems as tho I am walking in a London fog. I just am not too concerned about weather, or anything, just the time when I can be with you again!----.

Oh hell-----honey, I don't want you to feel bad but really I feel as tho I had lost the only thing I ever wanted—

You know, like a little boy who has lost his "mummy" in a crowded store he just stands there in blank wonderment trying to figure out why all he holds dear has deserted him----- I love you, "mummy" an' I need you, "mummy," I wuv you so-oo-o much!!—I a big baby, huh?—To let a little maneuver & a short separation disturb me so much, but---------

I'm in the U.S.O. right now waiting for the convoy to transport us back to the field, & they are playing the jukebox, they are playing "I'll be home for

Christmas"—and one of the lines in it is "if only in my dreams"—damn it------
It sure is easy to get morbid if you stop & think------.

Honey, you must forgive me for the inadequate Christmas Greetings I sent, but I couldn't get anything else & that is better than nothing at all!—(I guess!) Incidentally, the Fosters at Slocomb sent me a card & I never did send them one, did you send them one for us?

You see, darling, you also have to be my secretary in addition to being my wife!-----.

You ask if I hear from my mother or from Rose, yes I do, at least once a week—Perhaps the reason you haven't heard from Ro is because she took a short trip to Pittsburg & is making her arrangements to go to Miami Beach for the winter—

Ro is quite a socialite too & it does keep her rather occupied so you must forgive her------

Well, darling, I think I had better close now, I could write to you all nite, but the nights are rather brief here so-----------.

Be good, love me for I love you & I will write at my earliest opportunity----
> I love you,
> your
> Buddy

§

January 3, 1944

Sat.

My Dearest Wife:

Well, here is the first opportunity I have had to relax & write to my darling!---------God, it feels good to sit down & rest------.

I am at Lt. Brown's house. I've just finished taking a bath & a shave----. We checked in our "Canteen" at the warehouse & we would have showered in town, but we were in "fatigues" & it is not permissible to go about town in such attire—.

Darling, I haven't had a letter from you for 5 days but that is because our mail was held up again—

We finally have definite information about where we go to from maneuvers—it is Camp Butuer, North Carolina!!-------.

Now, honey, we should be there by the end of January, so if you get there about that time, it should work out just right!-----.

The place you should move to is Durham, NC (the home of Dukell.) It is not a large town, about 80,000 pop., but you shouldn't have too much difficulty in finding an apt. or room—.

Honey, you know what kind of place we'll want so as soon as you get there, go to "Travelers Aid," or U.S.O. or some such agency & inquire—o.k.?

Now about your transportation, I saw Sgt. Lyons (remember?) and he is having his car driven up to Durham by a wife of a boy that works in his office—

She is in Ozark, Ala. & you can get in touch with her by seeing Mr. Larry Dowling—He is on the Gas Ration Board at Ozark & is easy to find.

Now, honey, find out where you can locate Mrs. Johnson, the wife of this Sgt. in Lyon's office because she is going to get Sgt. Lyons car & drive it to Durham & it will be a good deal for you!!

At least, find out the circumstances & if it doesn't appeal to you why then go whichever way you think best—.

Incidentally, do you have sufficient luggage to transport your wardrobe? If you haven't, you better arrange for that too----------.

Well, darling, I hope to have you in my arms before another month goes by—I do hope I'm not disappointed!

Now, honey, if any of this is not very clear, tell me what you need to know in your next letter to me & I'll try to get you straightened out as much as possible.

Now, if I get in after you do why, you leave word at "Traveler's Aid" as to your whereabouts & I'll contact you----.

Well, darling, that is about all for now, so please write soon & let me know what puzzles you------.

I love you darling!
        Your
        "Buddy"

§

January 17, 1944
[Written on USO stationery]

Sun.
My Darling:

Firstly, please forgive me for not writing this week, but there wasn't the time or place!—It rained all week & the past 2 days have been nothing but snow & ice!—And I mean it is cold!—My fingers is so cold "Mummy" I can hardly write!!—but when I think just one more week & then this will all be over & we'll be together, it compensates for all the hardships I may have encountered in the last 2 months.

Honey, in one of your letters you ask me to get a 5 day pass & come & get you—That will be impossible darling & the only way you can get here is either by coming in Sgt. Lyon's car (as I wrote you) or to come by train or bus or however you can get there—.Now listen carefully, dearest, go to Durham & get in touch with the U.S.O. Traveler's Aid, they will help you get a place for us—

I don't know when I'll get there, but it will probably be about the end of January—I'll get in touch with "Traveler's Aid" and if you leave your address with them I'll be able to locate you—o.k.?—

About my clothes, darling, if you have room, bring it with you, if you haven't, leave it at home & we'll send for it-----------.

(Damn it's cold!!)

I got your four letters at one time & thank your mother for her letter, it was very sweet & I'll answer at my first opportunity-------------.

Well, dearest, I must go now as time is short & I have more work to do than I can even take care of-------

Love me, my darling, for I love you—(even if this handwriting does resemble the scratching of a moron).

    See you soon,
    your
    Buddy

§

Postmarked January 27, 1944

Mon. the 10th (just one more week)
My Dearest:

Had a letter from you today asking about how to go if you don't ride with Mrs. Johnson—well I think if you get there about the last week in January you'll be there the same time as me, so, leave for Durham anytime in that last week—o.k.? Had a letter from Rose, and she tells me she sent you a bracelet around Christmas time—Did you get it? She didn't put her name inside because a small card wouldn't fit, so if you got one & don't know who it was from, it was from Rose-----------

God, it's cold here these days, snow, mud & last nite it was below zero again—but I don't mind it knowing that each day brings you & I closer together----.

They are sending men on furlo this week, so chances are by the time we get to camp, we'll be in line for one also—Won't it be wonderful, darling?

The problem started this a.m. but I am sneaking this letter out—We closed the canteen yesterday, for good!—Lt. Brown has been pretty nice the past few weeks & he isn't a bad fellow at all even if he did get me "Hot" one day—Well, dearest, I better close now—Don't forget & tell me whether you got the bracelet from Rose or not-----

Your loving husband,
Buddy

§

Postcard from January 27, 1944

Tues. 8:30 p.m.
Dear Mom & Dad:

She has just arrived & we are doing nothing but looking fondly at each other—Thank you for keeping her so lovely—

Buddy

§

Audrey's Letters
to her mother and sister

August 13, 1943

Thursday –
Dearest Mother & All,

At last I'll try to let you hear from us. I thought I'd never get time. We're fine and surely hope all of you are, too.

We've been so busy–we moved Tuesday. I surely do like our room, but we still can't cook. It doesn't cost too much to eat in town, though.

Buddy has a terrible cold. It is some better but I surely was worried about him last night and the night before. He said tell you that he never enjoyed a day better than he did Sunday and that we're going back soon. I think he is almost wanting to start farming himself. He also said tell you that the lunch you prepared was terrific.

Tell Doris that I couldn't see the manager and the foreman don't know anything about the hiring but for her to come on and put in her application and I'm sure she'll get the job.

Must close now. Write often and come every time you can.

Lots & lots of love,
Audrey & Buddy

§

Undated

Saturday p.m. 1:30
Dearest Mother,

I will try to write you and the others again after getting settled.

Betty and I sure did have a time, cleaning this apartment. We washed every piece of dishes, which took us over five hours. We do have a nice place through. Three rooms, a living room, bedroom, kitchen and private bath. We have a gas stove to cook on and a nice refrigerator. Buddy had already rented it when I got here. He just happened to find it the Sunday before. Everyone here is looking for rooms. They're begging for rooms at any price. One of the Capt.'s in Buddy's outfit is paying $175 per. month for an apartment. We're paying $42 plus half the gas, electricity and telephone bill and buying our own coal for fuel.

If nothing happens Buddy and Charles get their furloughs Tuesday. I suppose all of us will stay here. We're afraid to turn the apartment loose and we can't keep paying for it and go anywhere on his furlough.

Mother, tell Doris that if she needs any material for shorts, I'll get her some. Tell her to write me and let me know what color she wants. They have every color you could want. Please tell me what size dress Olivia wears—2 or 3? I found the cutest little pink wool jumpers and white shirts that will fit her. I want to get her some. I also found some cute little print dresses for her. I can also get you some nice house dresses if you'll tell me the size. The stores here have everything.

This is a pretty town. It isn't much larger than Dothan, but there is so much more here. The only thing is that the weather is very changeable. When I got up this morning the sun was shining, now it's cloudy. One day it's freezing and the next day it's hot.

I have just finished washing. Buddy had quite a few pieces and so did I. I tried to wash everything, though.

Camp Butner is fourteen miles from here. It takes twenty minutes to go out there. It's just a nickel to call. Buddy calls me about 5 or 6 times a day.

Mother, take care of yourself. Write as often as you can. I'll write every chance I have. I'm going to work after Buddy's furlough. He doesn't want me to start before.

> *Lots of love,*
> *Annelle*

P.S. Kiss Olivia for me and tell the others I'll write them as soon as I can.

January 1944

Monday p.m. 12:45
Dearest Mother,

I do hope all of you are feeling all right. Buddy and I are fine, except we both have colds.

Betty and I have just finished cleaning the apartment and she is washing some of Charles' clothes he wore on maneuvers. I've already washed Buddy's. They were the dirtiest things I ever saw. They said they never did change their clothes but every three or four weeks.

Mother, I'm enclosing some bobby-pins for Doris. I think there are 30 on the card. I knew she needed some and I bought two cards. If that isn't enough I'll get her some more.

I hated to be in such a hurry, but I have to go to town and get something for dinner. I'm all messed up on the time here. They're an hour ahead of Ala. You don't have time to do anything much, except at night.

Take care of yourself. Tell all "hello" for me. I'll try to write again tomorrow.

> *Lots of love,*
> *Annelle*

P.S. I'm very anxious to hear from you—It's lonesome here without all of you.

§

January 1944

Tues. a.m.
Dearest Mother & All,

I do hope all of you are well. Buddy and I are all right—I'm having a little trouble with my stomach, but feel much better this morning so Buddy went back to camp.

Please forgive me Mother for not having written sooner. It's just one thing and then another. I was busy all day Saturday, preparing for guests, then Buddy was home Sunday and I like to have as much time with him as possible. Then Sunday night I was sick—Dr. Wilson, female specialist at Duke Hospital, said it was a cyst on one of my ovaries and had burst and one of my ovaries is enlarged. He says it isn't serious, but it can become serious. He told Buddy just what to do if I should have another attack. He also said it was possible that I'm pregnant, but I doubt it. If I am, he says I won't be able to carry it because it isn't in the womb, it's in the tube and it will burst very soon, but he says I have nothing to worry about. There were three doctors who examined me.

I do hope you're feeling much better and up with your work. Please don't worry about me because I'm all right.

I had a letter from Aunt Flora yesterday and she said they were all well.

I was very sorry to hear of Ruthi Mather's death. I know it must have been a terrible shock. I feel for all of them very much.

No, Mother, I didn't ask nor hint to Rose for the dresses. She had already asked me if I had any sisters or brothers and she was packing to go to Florida and she asked me if any of those would fit Annette or Olivia. I told her "yes" and she was very happy. She said she knew plenty of kids she could give them to, but their mother felt insulted and I told her that you wouldn't. She was very happy that they could use them.

Buddy leaves for maneuvers next week and then they'll have about two weeks here after they come back. I hate to see him go, but I know he has to.

Kiss little Olivia for me and tell all the others "hello" for me and I still say I'm going to write to all of them as soon as I can.

I just had to stop to answer the telephone. It was Buddy calling in to see how I felt.

I must close now. I'll write again tomorrow. Write as often as you can.
>   *Lots of Love,*
>   *Annelle*

P. S. I'm enclosing some coupons from Health Club Baking P. & Border's milk. Next time you write, let Olivia write me a letter.

§

January 27, 1944

Wed. p.m. 2:30
Dearest Mother,

I sure had a nice trip. Left Dothan at 2:00p.m. Monday—got in 6 Columbus, Ga. at 5:30 p.m., changed immediately for Atlanta, got there at 10:30 p.m. but had to wait until 2:30 a.m. Tuesday. Then I got a bus to Charlotte, N.C. and got there at 1:10 p.m. Tuesday, changed immediately and arrived in Durham at 7:45 last night.

Betty decided she couldn't stay in Chicago any longer so she and Charles went with Buddy to meet me at the bus terminal. She arrived yesterday at 5:00 p.m. and Charles met her. The bus was only three minutes late and Buddy was going crazy.

Charles and Buddy had already found and rented a nice apartment. We have a gas stove. Everything is really nice. The town is rather dirty looking, but the place we live is nice. Betty and I cook together. We have a private bath, refrigerator and everything. The apartment is $42 per month together.

I was rather tired when I got here, but we ate and I got a good night's rest. I didn't have any trouble at all. In fact, I enjoyed it. Met some nice ladies on the bus. Just as we drove out of Charlotte though, a car ran over a little boy and killed him and I was still nervous from that when I got here. I checked my luggage and all of it got here last night. Two came in with me, then the other came in at 9:45 and the porter called us. I got it this morning.

Tell all of them "hello" for me. I would write to each one, but haven't had a chance to even unpack yet.

My address is: 304 Markham St., Durham.

Must close now and go mail this. I wrote three cards along the way, but didn't have time to mail them.

I miss all of you. Take care of yourself and don't work too hard.

Write soon.

> *Lots of Love,*
> *Annelle*

P.S. Buddy gets his furlough Feb. 1. Hope to have enough money to get back to Dothan and keep our apartment, too.

§

January 29, 1944
[Written on USO stationery]

Sun. Night

Dearest Mother & All,

I do hope all of you are well. Buddy and I are fine. I went to a doctor Saturday to have this mole removed. He told me it was good that I was having it done now. It was infected. He is going to take it off tomorrow. I'll be glad when it's over.

I suppose Buddy will be leaving in a few weeks. They're on alert now. It may be 90 days—or less. I can hardly stand the thoughts of him going over, but, of course, I can only hope & pray for the best.

I'm sending Jimmie three boxes of air-rifle shots. I just happened to find them. I hope he can use them.

I sent a pattern for Doris' gym suit. I hope you got it and the material. It's a cute pattern. I also sent her some lipstick and some buttons in the pattern. I hope the lipstick is the right shade.

Betty is very happy that I'm going to California. We'll go by way of Chicago and stay a day or so with Rose. Betty told me she would go with me to Mother Frees' in Venice, Calif. She also asked me to stay a day or so with her before I go.

Did you get the dresses Rose sent? If so, how did Annette like them? Could she wear them?

We're at the USO. Nothing much to do. Buddy painted an 11x14 picture of me—It's a very good one. In fact, it flatters me.

Mother, I must say goodbye now. Please write as often as you can. I enjoy hearing from you—I miss all of you so much.

> *Love,*
> *Annelle*

P.S. I sent 4 stamps in one letter.

§

February 23, 1944

Tuesday

Dearest Mother,

I do hope all of you are well. Buddy and I are all right. He's having to work rather hard.

He had a show last night and will have one Thursday night, a quiz program Friday and a show for the prisoners in Raleigh Saturday. Then in about two weeks he goes on Virginia maneuvers for 18 days. They carry 120 lb. packs, climb 4400 ft. high and use mules for other equipment.

I had the mole removed yesterday. It sure did hurt, but it hasn't bothered me since. Dr. Tyler told me to keep it dressed every two days and to come back for him to see it in about three weeks.

The weather here is so rainy. It's very changeable. Yesterday was a beautiful day and when I got up at 7:00 it was raining.

Tell Daddy and the others "hello" for me. I'd sure like to see all of you. When I read your letters, it's almost like talking to you. I enjoy them so much.

The USO's here have sewing machines. Betty and I are going to buy some material and she is going to make her some dresses—I'm going to make Olivia some little print ones.

Mother, it's almost time for Buddy—I must stop and make him some dinner.

Write as often as you can.

Lots of love,

Annelle

P.S. Tell Jimmie I'll mail his air-rifle shots tomorrow—the post office was closed today for Washington's birthday.

§

February 24, 1944

Wed. night

Dearest Mother & all,

I received your letter just a few minutes after I had mailed you one. I also got one from Aunt Les. She said all of them are well.

You said you hadn't received those dresses you should have by now. I insured them. I also hope you'll get the material for Doris's shorts, the buttons, pattern, lipstick and air-rifle shots.

I'd give anything to see all of you and little Olivia. What words can she say? I wish I could hear her. I'm afraid she'll always have to have her bottle. I wish you could have her picture made and send me one. Speaking of pictures, I want you to keep those pictures of Buddy until I ask for them and most likely that will be after the war's over.

Tell Daddy, Doris, Joe, Jimmie, Annette and Olivia "hello" for me and I'd like very much to see and hear from them. Let me know what Olivia says in answer to that.

Mother, since I just wrote you last night, I don't know anything else, so I'll say goodnight. Write as often as you can.

I sure hope you're feeling all right.

Lots of love,

Annelle

March 1, 1944

Wednesday p.m.

Dearest Mother & All,

I will try to answer your much appreciated letters I received while I was gone. I have several more to answer. I had ten when I got home.

I do hope all of you are well. We're o.k. Buddy went back to camp last night. It seemed like the time flew while we were on furlough. His outfit is going on maneuvers in Virginia next week. They'll be gone for three weeks, then they'll come back here and prepare for amphibious training, then I'm afraid they're going overseas. Buddy thinks so, too. I'm going to work as soon as I can. When Buddy goes over, I suppose I'll be going to California to stay with Mother Frees and work in the defense plant where Mannie works.

Mother, I sent the dresses that Rose gave to you. You should be getting them in a few days. I also got the material for Doris' shorts. I got 3 ½ yards. I couldn't find a solid blue in good material, so I'm sending blue stripe. It's good material—I hope she'll like it. I'm sorry I couldn't find any tennis shoes. I couldn't even get them in Chicago.

Rose gave me some very pretty hose. She's getting some nylons and is going to send me some. All her friends were so nice to us. When we started to leave, they gave us candy and cigarettes. Every night we were there, we went somewhere. Rose gave us seventy-five dollars to spend and then gave us enough to pay our rent for two weeks. She was sick the last three days we were there. We had everything to eat. When we started home she gave us some crab meat, tuna fish, olives, filet fish and quite a few other things.

Mother, I miss all of you so much. You can't imagine. I'd give anything to see you. Please tell them all "hello" for me and kiss little Olivia for me. I can just see her now.

I must close now and answer some of the others. Please write as often as you can. Don't work too hard.

> *Lots of love,*
> *Annelle*

P.S. Tell Doris I'll get her lipstick. And I think I can get some gum for you. Mother, if you can, please send me a no. 3 ration book and Buddy's cigarette lighter.

§

March 6, 1944
[Written on "Annelle Frees" stationery]

Sat. P.M.

Dearest Mother and All,

I do hope all of you are well and feeling good tonight. Buddy and I are fine. He is so tired though, he can't see. He worked all afternoon on some cartoons for the officers' party. He's sleeping now.

I went out to camp today. The Under Secretary of War was out for a demonstration and we were planning to go, but Buddy had to draw all those cartoons. I don't think they had any men killed; several were hurt.

I told you that Buddy did a show for the prisoners at Raleigh, didn't I? Anyway, he did and one of the boys sent him the most beautiful billfold I ever saw and he gave it to me. It is handmade with drawings on the outside and has his name cut in the leather on the inside. If it had been sold it would have sold for $15. He enclosed a card and told Buddy how much he appreciated and enjoyed the show.

How are Annette and Olivia? I'd give anything to see them as well as the rest of you.

I went to see about the job at the hospital, but didn't take it because they wanted a girl who would be there permanently. I'm going Monday to see about a job at one of the tobacco plants.

There isn't much news. Buddy's leaving next Friday for Virginia maneuvers. They'll be there until about the first of April. They come back here and stay until the 15th of April, then they'll be on their way overseas. Mother, it's the hardest thing I've ever had to face. Sometimes I feel as though I just can't bear to see him leave, but I know he has to go and I'll have to do the best I can. I know he'll get over just in time to be one of the first to go into the new invasion. If I just knew that he would come back just as he goes over, it wouldn't be so bad, but there's always the thought that he might be among the ones who don't come back.

I'm getting so nervous, I can't talk about it anymore.

Please write every time you can. Take care of yourself and don't work too hard.

Tell Daddy and the others "hello" for us. Give them our love.

> *Goodnight,*
> *Lots of love,*
> *Annelle*

March 7, 1944
[Written on "Annelle Frees" stationery]

Mon. P.M.

Dearest Mother,

I just got your letter a few minutes ago. I was very glad to hear from you again. Tell Doris and Annette that I enjoyed their letters very much, too.

There isn't much news. Buddy and I are fine. The place where the mole was, is all gone. It didn't give me any trouble at all. My stomach hasn't bothered me since. It wasn't anything.

I'm rather down in the dumps today. I've been walking the streets (until it started raining) looking for a job—I can't find anything. They wouldn't even take my application at the tobacco plant. With worrying about finding a job and the thought that Buddy will be leaving the 15th of April is driving me crazy. We're already two days late with the rent and it looks as though my check isn't coming. I have $46 in my purse and that's all the money we have. I suppose there is a way out. We have $50 in the bank, but that's part of my transportation money. Oh! well things will work out, I'm sure.

How is little Olivia? I'd give anything to see her. Please kiss her for me.

I suppose that's all for this time. I'll write more when I'm in a better mood. I'm glad you have your garden started. I know it's pretty.

Please give mine and Buddy's love to all.

> *Lots of Love,*
> *Annelle*

P.S. I'm enclosing a few stamps.

§

March 17, 1944
[Written on "Annelle Frees" stationery]

Thurs. P.M.

Dearest Mother,

I received your's and Doris' letters and thank you both so much for them. I was very happy to hear from you again.

I started working today at a cafeteria. It's a very nice place. I'll make $12.50 per week plus two meals a day. I'm so tired now though that I can't move.

Yes, I wrote and thanked Rose for the clothes and she said she was very glad they could use them.

I had a letter from Buddy yesterday and he says it's rather cold there, but beautiful scenery. He's very anxious to get back here, though. He'll be back in two weeks. I can hardly wait to see him.

Give our love to Daddy and the others. We're sure like to see all of you. I may get down for a couple of days before I go to California but I don't know yet. I'll let you know.

Kiss little Olivia for me. I'd give anything to see her. I know she's almost grown.

Mother, if I don't write as often as I should like, you'll understand. I'm working from 10:00 A.M until 8:00 P.M. and I have to write Buddy, do my washing, pressing, etc. at night.

Please write as often as you can. Lots of Love,

Annelle

§

March 23, 1944
[To her sister. Written on "Annelle Frees" stationery]

Wed. Night

My Dearest little sister,

How is the "sweetest little girl in the world" tonight? I do hope you and the others are all right. I would give anything to see you—just to get to hold you and rock you to sleep. You are the sweetest little sister I ever saw.

Are you sweet to Annette, Joe, Jimmie and Doris? You must be, because they love you so much and they look after you. Tell them "hello" for Buddy and me. Please give Mother and Daddy a great big hug and kiss for us, too. We both love all of you so very much.

I'm sorry Precious that I haven't written before now, but sister has been very busy with her new job. I like it fine, though.

Buddy will be back next Tuesday. I can hardly wait to see him.

I may come home for a few days after he leaves. Would you be glad to see me and would you let me rock you to sleep—just once? Please do.

I love you, little doll. I would like to write more, but I'm so tired. I just got off work and got home and wrote Buddy and it's passed nine now.

So be sweet and write me a long letter.

Much love to all of you.

Your sister, Annelle

§

April 7, 1944
[Written on "Annelle Frees" stationery]

Thurs. Eve.

Dearest Mother, Daddy & All,

I received Daddy's card and appreciated it very much, although I must admit I was surprised. I also received your letter, card and the clothes. Thank you so much, Mother.

I'm sorry Aunt Les didn't get the bag in time. I sent it as soon as I got the letter. I would like to use it again when I start home, if she doesn't mind.

About my going home. I don't exactly when I will go. It may be three or four weeks or it may be longer. They don't know exactly when they're leaving. I'll go and stay a week or so with you and then I'll leave for the coast. Betty isn't going to wait for me because she's going through Kansas to see some of Charles' people. Mildred Elliott is going from here to Dothan with me. She's staying with her mother a few days then she's going to New York to stay with Doris' folks. I'll come as soon as Buddy leaves, but I'm praying that he doesn't have to go.

I'm sorry that little Olivia has been sick. I'm glad she's better. Sure wish I could see her and the rest of you, too.

Poor little Buddy has been sick again, but he won't go to the hospital. He's afraid they'll think he's trying to "play off." He was very sick last night and the day before, though.

We had some pictures made last Thursday night. It will be about three weeks before we can get them, but when we do get them, I'll send you one. They're 8"x10". We are having six made.

We had a letter from Buddy's brother, Dave. He sent us a picture of him and his wife and their baby. They're all so happy that I'm going out there. Dave said, "We'll sure look after your Honey 'til you get back." Rose is going out there in May and it might be that I could go along with her. She also wrote us a long, sweet letter.

That's about all the news. Must close. Please take care of yourself. Give our love to all.

Lots of love,
Annelle

§

April 16, 1944
[Written on USO stationery]

Thursday

Dearest Mother & All,

I received yours and Doris' letters this morning. Thank you so much for it. I surely enjoy hearing from you.

I do hope all of you are fine. Buddy and I are well and happy. We're enjoying ourselves while we're together. We don't know how long he'll be here.

I'm glad Daddy has gotten started with his planting and sure hope the weather will permit him to finish as soon as possible. I know you're eager to get the crops started. I'll bet you have a nice garden. I sure would like to have one of your good home-cooked meals. It's so tiresome eating out. It just isn't like home-cooking.

I'm glad the litter of pigs are growing. They can't get too fat to eat. Mother, I'm so happy that you have some little biddies. I do hope you can raise them for eating and laying.

I'd sure enjoy some good sugar-cured ham. If you could send just a little bit. I can almost taste it now.

I know Olivia is beautiful by now. I would give anything to see her. I probably wouldn't know her, she's grown so much. Kiss her for us. Tell Daddy, the boys, Doris and little Annette "hello" for us and we'd sure like to see them.

Poor little Buddy is working again tonight. He and Charles both. It's something all the time.

I was surely sorry to hear Frances was sick, but I'm glad she's better. When she's able, I'd like for her to write to me. I had a letter from Nadine a few days ago. She said Charlotte had been sick, but was better.

It's too bad about Truman Rollins. I knew him and he seemed to be a nice boy. I'm so sorry for his folks.

I want to tell you a little secret, but don't get alarmed. Buddy and I are tick-led over it. I'm not sure yet, but I think I'm going to have a baby.

Mother, I have to write to Edna, Katherine and Aunt Les, so please excuse short letter. I'll try to write again in a day or two.

Please write me a long letter. I love you.

Annelle

§

April 25, 1944
[Written on USO stationery]

Tues. P.M.

Dear Folks,

I received your letter and was very happy to hear from you again. It had been so long since you wrote.

I hope you're well and not working too hard. Buddy and I are fine. We're trying to forget our troubles and be happy while we can. Our time is so short. These last three months have just flown by. I hardly know where they've gone.

Doris told me that Frances is married. Well, I can't say that I'm surprised. I do hope she'll be very happy. Where is she living now?

Mother, I suppose I'll be home in about two weeks. I won't have very long to stay. I want to get to Calif. while Rose is there. She arrived there today and will be there until the 21st of May.

Have you gotten Olivia's pictures yet? Be sure to save me one. I know she must have grown so much and I know she is still beautiful.

Mother, are you sick? I hope not. It's been so long since I heard from you. Did it scare you so when I told you I'm going to have a baby? I hope not.

Must close now. Write soon.

Lots of love,
Annelle

§

May 18, 1944
[Written on Annelle Frees stationery]

Wed. P.M.

Dearest Mother & All,

I arrived Sunday night at 7:45. Rose and Dave met me. I had good connections all the way. I didn't have any trouble at all.

California is wonderful. It's still rather cool, but maybe by next month it'll be warmer.

How is everyone? Fine, I do hope. I miss you very much, Mother. Maybe with us all praying this will soon be over with and we can be together again.

I just love Mom and Pa. They're both so sweet to me. Mannie, Dave and Helen are very sweet, too.

Rose is leaving Sunday. She's been so sweet to me. They can't seem to do enough.

I may start to work for 20th Century-Fox pictures. I hope so.

That's all for now, Mother—I'll write more next time.

Answer soon.

  Lots of Love,
  Annelle

P.S. Save everyone a big kiss for me.

§

May 23, 1944

Dearest Mother & All,

How are you and the others? I do hope you're well and happy. We're well and enjoying ourselves.

Rose left Sunday. They may come out here to live. I hope they can.

Mom and Pa are very sweet to me. They won't let me do anything.

I went to look for a job this morning. I found one as a sales lady—$18 per week, but they said I shouldn't take it. It doesn't pay enough. Jobs are plentiful. I'll get something. I'm just waiting for my application at 20th Century-Fox to go through.

Kiss little Olivia for me and give the others my love. I'd sure like to hear from you.

I haven't heard from Buddy yet. I called Betty yesterday and she said she hasn't heard from Charles, either. They must be on their way over. I just hope and pray Buddy will come back safely.

I have a nice, big bedroom with a nice closet. Pa made me a beautiful bed lamp.

How is your garden? I do hope you're getting plenty of vegetables to eat. I know you are. What about the crop? I know it keeps all of you so busy that you can't think. I think of you so much. Please don't work too hard, Mother. Don't worry about me. I'm fine and like Calif. very much. It's much cooler here than I thought. I have to wear a heavy coat all the time.

How are the children doing in school? They should be out in about a week or two.

How are Doris and Seal? Ha!! Tell her to tell Seal "hello" for me.

Did you get the telegram? I sent it as soon as I saw Rose—she sent it for me. Please write every time you can and so will I.

> *Lots of Love,*
> *Annelle*

P.S. Wasn't there something you asked me to get? If so, tell me again and I'll get it—with pleasure.

Don't worry about me going too close to the ocean—it's too scary looking.

§

May 30, 1944

Monday
My Dearest Mother,

I received your letter today and thank you so much. It was the next thing to talking. It was just the kind of letter I like to get—with all the news.

I'm so sorry that Olivia still has that breaking out on her. I hope it soon goes away.

I'm glad you heard from James Edward and that he is well. How is Frances? So Aunt Ollie is going to visit Mary Esther.

I'm glad you have some new little biddies. I sure hope you have good luck with them.

I'm sure glad John doesn't have to go to the army. I know Nadin is happy, too.

At last you got your honey and there wasn't much.

I would be so happy for Thelma, especially, if Henry gets a furlough. I knew she's thrilled to death.

I think you did have a house full of company. That's right, though—when it rains—it pours.

I know you're glad school is out and I'm happy for all of you. Don't any of you work too hard, though.

I'm working for the telephone co. and it's rather interesting, but a little confusing. I know it'll be much easier after I get used to it.

I haven't heard from Buddy yet, but I hope it won't be long, though. I'm glad you wrote to him—Every letter will mean so much to him.

Betty spent Saturday night with me. We didn't do anything but talk. It was so good to see her. She has asked me to stay with her a week from Saturday. I'm going and we're going into Hollywood with her Mother and Daddy.

Please give my love to Daddy, Doris, Joe, Jimmie, Annette and Olivia. Give you a kiss for me.

Write every time you can and so will I.

  Lots & Lots of Love,
  Annelle

§

June 1, 1944

Dearest Mother & All,

I do hope all of you are well and not working too hard. We're all fine.

The weather here is beautiful.

I haven't heard from Buddy yet, but I hope I will hear soon. I'm so anxious to hear from him. It seems so long. Since I'm working, the time just flies, though. Honestly, I just don't know where this week has gone.

I had a letter from Nadine and she said the children had been sick, but were better now.

Today was ten months ago Buddy and I were married. It seems only yesterday. I wish it was and we could have all that time together again. No, I suppose that's wrong, but I'd sure give anything to see him.

How is little Olivia? I do hope she's better. Kiss her for me and tell Daddy and the others "hello" for me. I'd like to hear from them.

Mother, please take care of yourself and don't work too hard. I do hope you feel good. You know you always try to do too much.

There's not much news. I wish there was.

I'll try to write two or three times a week if I possibly can. If I don't, just don't worry about me. I'm usually rather tired when I get home from work and I just sit.

Goodnight, sleep tight and don't worry.

I love all of you.

> *Lots and Lots of Love,*
> *Annelle*

§

June 20, 1944
[Written on Annelle Frees stationery]

Thursday

My Dearest Mother,

I just received your's, Doris and Aunt Ollie's letters. I was very happy to hear from all of you. I hardly know what to say about the things I've been told. I've always heard, when it rains, it pours—but I've just learned the full meaning. First, Buddy leaves—then I'm away from home and on top of that, which seems quite a bit, then I hear that a person I always put so much confidence in, tells everything they can to ruin my life and to drive me insane. I suppose that everyone has troubles, but in the past two months, it seems as though, I'm getting part of someone else's. If I could "just laugh it off" as some people can— but I can't. Maybe I'm too serious. Mother, there's no use denying—it's hurt and worried me so much. I try to laugh and be gay while Buddy's gone. At night I pray with all my heart for his safe return and for courage, faith and strength. I'm glad you've told me. I don't want to be "fooled along." In the evenings when I come in from work, I'm rather tired, but in high spirits, hoping I'll have a letter from Buddy—only to be disappointed—hearing such things that seem impossible for people to make. There's one thing I'm thankful for—the thought that I have the most wonderful Mother and husband in the world and to have enough faith in Buddy to know that he's broad-minded enough—not to believe such things. She can say anything about me that she wants to, but especially while Buddy's away, she better not say anything about him.

I do hope you're all well. I hope you're feeling much better by now. We're all o.k.—just waiting to hear from Buddy again.

Sometimes, it seems that life holds nothing for me, but then I know I'm only "crazy" because I have everything, the sweetest family in the world and the most wonderful husband in the world.

I know you're tired of hearing my troubles—you have plenty of your own, but thank you, Mother, for listening—I feel much better after talking to you.

Kiss Olivia for me—I'd give anything to see her and the rest of you. Give my love to the others.

Write as often as you can and I will do the same. I must stop and write my daily letter to Buddy. Today is his birthday—bless his heart—I wonder how he's spending it.

Goodnight, Dearest Mother.

> Lots & Lots of Love,
> Annelle

§

June 6, 1944
[Written on Annelle Frees stationery]

Monday

My Dearest Mother,

I just received your letter and thank you so much for it.

We're all well—Mom was sick last week, but she's better now. She worries so much about Buddy. I haven't had a letter from him yet—I'm still waiting—trying to be patient. It seems so long, though.

Mother, so often I've thought of what you've said—"There's always a silver lining"—and I'm just praying for it in this case. God help it to be very soon.

Yes, I like my work very much. I welcome night, though, so I can get to sit a little. I work from 8:00 A.M.—5:00 P.M. An hour for lunch and two 15 minute rest periods. All the people are very nice to me. All my work is walking—I deliver and collect mail from all the offices, trim cylinders from Dictaphones. Do some typing and a few other things.

I wrote Aunt Les, sent her black bag and a picture of me and Buddy. I'm going to write everyone as soon as I have time. It seems all I do is eat, sleep—get up and work. I work 5 ½ days a week. Very nice set up.

I'm going into Los Angeles Saturday and I'm going to look for the bed rollers and oil cloth. I'm here and you're there so you can't stop me from getting it if I can find it.

Of all things, Mr. & Mrs. Clark are separated. That's something.

I'm glad Joe and Jimmie get some clothes—They needed them.

I wrote little Annette a letter. I hope she got it.

I'm glad Doris got to go to stay with Tom and Lucille for awhile. She needed the change.

Tell Daddy "hello" for me and not to work too hard. Kiss little Pumpkin for me—and give you a big hug.

Yes Mother, I was telling Mom yesterday that yesterday was a year ago I graduated. It seems almost impossible.

Mother, I'm very fortunate, but, still I'd rather have Buddy than anything. The whole world before me would be nothing without him.

Goodnight, my Dearest "Mummy". Sleep tight.

I love you,

> *Lots of Love,*
> *Annelle*

§

June 9, 1944
[Written on Annelle Frees stationery]

Dearest Mother & All,

I do hope you and the others are well. We are and enjoying ourselves.

One of the girls from the office came home with me to stay overnight.

Dave got his vacation this week and he and Helen came over and spent the night last night.

I haven't heard from Buddy yet—I'm still praying that I'll hear from him. I do hope he's all right—and will be the same when he gets back.

Kiss little Olivia for me and tell the others "hello" for me and not to work too hard.

Nadine told me Daddy had a tooth pulled—I do hope he's feeling all right.

—Which reminds me, I looked for something for Father's Day—I'm going to get him something Saturday, but don't tell him----

Mother, take care of yourself and don't work too hard. I think of you so much.

Write every time you can, I do enjoy hearing from you.
Must close—Goodnight, "Mummy."
　　　Lots & Lots of Love,
　　　Annelle

§

June 10, 1944
[Written on Annelle Frees stationery]

Monday Night
My Dearest Mother,
　　I just received your letter and thank you so much. I always enjoy hearing from you so much. Thank you also for enlightening me on things. It's true, you never know who you can trust.
　　I do hope you're all well. We are. Mom's up and feeling much better. She still goes on cleaning and cooking. Always having dinner hot when Mannie and I get home from work. Doing everything to make us comfortable and happy.
　　I had a letter from Buddy Saturday and today. They were very sweet. He had a pass the other day. He said Sunday didn't seem like Sunday at all because I wasn't there and he missed me so much.
　　I'm sending a picture I had made. It isn't good. I had some made for Buddy. He wanted some small ones.
　　I had a new experience yesterday (Sunday). We had four tremblers (earthquakes). The first wasn't hard, but the others were. I didn't know what was happening at first and I was afraid, but I knew what to expect the next time and it gave me a good ride. Mom, Pa and I were sitting on the couch and—all at once, everything was shaking—Just don't worry, they're fun. They were the first in three years.
　　Take care of yourself, Mother. Don't worry and please don't work too hard.
　　Kiss little Olivia for me and give my love to Daddy, Doris, Joe, Jimmie, Annette and give you a nice, big hug.
　　Goodnight—write every time you can.
　　　Lots of Love,
　　　Annelle

§

June 13, 1944
[Written on Annelle Frees stationery]

Monday

My Dearest Mother & All,

I received your letter today and thank you so much. It sure helped my feeling. Today being Monday and dreary—with no word from Buddy, your letters surely did make a brighter day for me.

I wrote Mrs. Fussell and asked her to send me Mary Lou's address. I got it today and also a letter from Edna. They were all fine.

I stayed with Betty Saturday night. She sure did a wonderful job entertaining me. She took me to dinner at a French restaurant. Then she took me to the Biltmore (the theatre where she first saw Buddy. It was the first time I can truthfully say, I laughed and really enjoyed myself since Buddy's been gone. Her Mother and Daddy are wonderful. They were so nice to me. They have a beautiful home. Her Mother asked me how I liked it here and I told her I like it. She said, "I'm so glad you do—I was so worried that you wouldn't be satisfied." She just begged me to come back to stay with Betty, that Betty was so much more satisfied when we're together. Sunday afternoon we went into Chinatown. I wanted to get you some pieces of China, but oh! is it expensive. I'm still going to get at least one.

Mother, I'm sending Daddy's Father's Day gift. It isn't much, but it's about all I could do. I hope he likes them. Some day, I'll make it up to both of you. I'm also sending Olivia a little dress and a pair of panties. I hope they fit. If the panties fit, I'll get some more. I know you'll have to hem up the dress, but I thought it was a cute thing.

So Olivia calls Annette, Janie? That's cute. I'd give anything to see her and the rest of you.

Tell Doris her letter was very sweet, just as yours was. I do enjoy hearing from you so much. Give my love to Olivia, Annette, Doris, Joe, Jimmie and Daddy. Tell them to write when they can. Just continue to pray with me for Buddy's and the other boys return.

I'm enclosing some stamps for you.

I must close now. Goodnight my dearest Mother.

Please don't work too hard. I know you have so much to do, although I'm so glad the crop isn't so grassy.

Goodnight everyone and God bless you. I love every one of you.
    Lots & Lots of Love,
    Annelle

§

June 17, 1944
[Written on Annelle Frees stationery]

Friday Night
My Darling Mother,
    I am so happy—I just couldn't wait any longer to write. I had two letters from Buddy today. Mom started telling me before I got upstairs.
    He said he's well both physically and mentally. He's somewhere in England. He says it's beautiful—They talk quite different than us. I was so happy to hear from him. He asked me to have a small picture made for him—I'm going to have one made tomorrow.
    I do hope all of you are well. We are and I feel especially good after reading Buddy's letters.
    Give my love to Daddy, Doris, Joe, Jimmie, Annette and Olivia. Tell them I miss them and would like very much to see all of you. Some day before long—if I have my way, you're coming out to see me.
    I'm still working and still like it fine. I don't make too much, but the main thing is that my time is well occupied.
    I hope you got the package in time for Daddy to get his little present—It isn't too much, but just something to let him know that I remembered.
    Mother, please take care of yourself and please don't work too hard.
    There isn't much news—write as often as you can and I will do the same.
    I love all of you—
    Lots & Lots of Love,
    Annelle

§

June 22, 1944
[Written on Annelle Frees stationery]

Saturday

My Dearest Mother,

I received your's and Doris' letters and thank you so much. I'm always so glad to hear from you. I write every time, but I don't write as often as I would like to.

I do hope you're all well. We are and having some of the most beautiful weather now. It sure seems good, too, for it's been rather cold. I'm just beginning to know what California weather is like. Nice and warm, with a breeze. Always.

Well, another week almost gone. I just got in from work at 12:30. We work 'til noon on Saturday.

Mother, I looked for some little panties for Olivia and didn't see any in Santa Monica (that's where I work) but I'm going into Los Angeles in a little while and I'm going to look there. I'm almost sure they have some there.

Well, I could hardly believe my eyes when I read Doris' letter. It hurt so much to know that I loved so much. If that's the way she wants it, believe me, she'll never be bothered with me or Buddy anymore. I didn't think she could say such things, but just forget it. Don't let it bother you. I'm going to forget it.

Mom just went down to lie on the beach. She's been in all week and when she doesn't get out, she just worries so much, she stays sick almost all the time. Pa is so good to her and the cutest thing you ever saw. If there's anything I want, he makes it his business to go out and get it.

Must close. Write every time you can. I love every one of you. Give my love to all.

Lots of Love,
Annelle

§

June 22, 1944
[Written on Annelle Frees stationery]

Wednesday

My Dearest Mother & All,

I received your letters yesterday and please forgive me for not having answered last night. I hope this will be the same.

I've had several letters from Buddy. He seems to be satisfied in England and that makes me very happy. They get passes and get to go to dances, so that gives them a little rest, I'm so happy they had.

I had a letter from Aunt Les and she said she got the bag and the picture of Buddy and me and she seems to like it very much. She also asks for Buddy's address, so I answered and sent it to her.

I got a letter from Doris while she was in Montgomery. She said she's having a wonderful time and I'm so happy she got the chance to go. She sure deserves to. She's so sweet and good to work. I wish you could have gone.

Tell Daddy, I'm sure sorry he hasn't been feeling good. I hope he's better now.

I know Olivia was happy to get the little ring and dress. I know she's darling to wear them. Today is her birthday, so give her an extra big kiss for me.

I've started my other check from Buddy. I also filled out the card to have my other check changed.

Dave and Helen are taking me out Saturday night, we're going dancing. They're so nice. They said they know it's lonesome, just sitting around on Saturday night, so they're going to take me out.

The days sure go by so fast. I hardly know where they go. Tomorrow is little Buddy's birthday. I'd give anything to be with him. Maybe on his next one, we will be. I pray every night that it will be very soon that all the mothers and wives can have their sons and husbands home again.

Write often.

> *Lots & Lots of Love,*
> *Annelle*

§

June 23, 1944

Saturday
My Dearest Mother,

I received your much appreciated letter and thank you so much. I always enjoy reading your letters. They mean so much to me. It's just like talking to you.

I hope you're all well and not working too hard. I think of you every day, knowing how you're running your legs off—to do this thing and that.

I had a letter from Buddy yesterday. It was a V. Mail letter, dated June 5. It wasn't photographed—I don't know why. He's still well. They (he and Charles) went bicycle riding the other day.

Kiss little Olivia for me and give the others my love. I would write to each one, separately, but I'm always busy.

I'm sending Olivia a little pinafore and blouse. I hope it fits. I also found a nice looking piece of viol—or long cloth. I'm sending 3 ½ yards for a dress for you. I hope you like it. I thought it was pretty. I was going to send buttons, but they wanted $.25 each for plain ones. They get a fortune for everything here, but they have beautiful clothes.

I'm going to stay overnight with Dave and Helen tonight. I hardly get home before I'm off again. It keeps me going around in circles.

Mother, there just isn't any news today. I'll write again soon and maybe there will be more to say.

I received Doris' and Aunt Ollie's letters with yours. You can tell her I received it and was glad to get it. I'll write to you only—you're the only one I can trust—outside you, Daddy and the others—I won't write anyone.

Write soon.

> *Lots & Lots of Love,*
> *Annelle*

§

July 5, 1944

Thursday
Darling little Sister,

I received your very sweet and much appreciated letter today and thank you so much. I hope everyone is feeling well. Buddy and I are fine—I didn't feel good yesterday, but I'm fine today.

Darling, I will do my best about getting a dress for you. If I had the money I could send you some beautiful things. The money is the only thing that holds me back—However, I'll do my best. I'll look tomorrow and maybe I can pay a little every week and get something. Don't be mad, darling, if I can't get it right away. I'll tell you something—Everything is so expensive out here and Buddy and I have to think twice before we buy anything. We're trying to save money to buy a house and he works night and day almost and I just don't have the heart to spend money as freely as I would like. Now please, darling, if I've hurt your feelings, I'm very sorry, but that's the way things are for us right now. As I said though—I'll do my best!!

About going home, Honey—I wish I knew—you couldn't want me to come any worse than I want to, but if only you could know how impossible it is for us to think of it now.

Darling, I know you're going to hate me for writing such an awful letter and I'll probably hate myself in the morning, but I just wanted to tell you. Just wait, honey, if we ever get started—you'll have plenty of things.

Kiss everyone for us and give them our love and please don't hate me.

I love you,

Your loving Sis & Brother Annelle & Buddy

§

July 6, 1944

Thursday

July 6th

My Dearest Mother,

I received your very sweet letter today and needless to say, I was very happy to hear from you. Even though I didn't answer as soon as I have finished reading it as I usually do, I hope you will forgive me. I just haven't felt in the mood to write today at all, even though I wrote Buddy as I do every day.

I hope all of you are well and not working too hard. I know you have so much to do, though.

Mother, I don't know why but everything seems so strange. It seems as though I've gone my last mile. I've felt all day as though I'm waiting for something that's bad news. There seems that I don't have any future to hope for any longer. I wish I could snap out of it, I'm so miserable—something I can't explain. So many people are being killed—within the past week, there's been three coal mine fires, two train accidents, a fire from a circus and so many killed over the 4th. I took a walk, trying to forget everything, but it's still there. I feel like crying my eyes out. Maybe it's because I miss Buddy so much. I've been hearing from him often but it seems that if I have to wait another day to see him, I'll go crazy. He's so sweet and good—and nobody knows how I love him and to think they snatch him off into such!! Mother, it just hurts beyond words. If he was mean to me or did things he shouldn't maybe I could say he deserves it, but he doesn't. He never hurt anybody—He's too tender hearted!! I feel like dying—or something. I just don't have any desire to live while he's away!!

Please forgive dearest Mother. I just had to tell somebody and of course a child always runs to its Mother first, I suppose.

Tell little Annette and Doris that I'd give anything if I had the money to buy them a dress. I love to buy for all of you, but frankly—right now I have exactly 12 cents—Betty asked me over for the weekend, but I don't have enough to get over there—so it goes. Someday I hope I can buy them anything they want. Kiss little Olivia for me and give all of them my love.

Mother, if you know where to get my birth certificate, would you please write for it? I have to have it before I can get a job.

I think I've grumbled enough for this time. Please don't worry about what I said. A good night's rest will cure me—I just had to get it off my mind. I'm beginning to feel better already.

Sleep tight "mummy"—I love all of you.

Write soon.

> Lots & Lots of Love,
> Annelle

§

July 11, 1944
[Written on Annelle Frees stationery]

Tuesday

My Dearest Mother,

How are you and the others today? I hope you're well and not working too hard. I haven't had a letter from you for quite a few days. I just hope you're not sick.

I haven't heard from Buddy this week. I hope and pray that he is well and safe. I hope I hear from him tomorrow.

I went job hunting yesterday. Not too much luck, but a little encouragement. Several managers of department stores told me to come back Wednesday—they might be able to use me. Pa suggested that I take a business course and he'll pay for it. I may do that—I know it would help me to get a better paying job. Did you write for my birth certificate yet?

Betty and I had dinner in L.A. at Melody Lane Saturday night, then went to a show to see "Standing Room Only" and "Show Business." Good shows. I sure enjoy being out and to just forget everything.

There just isn't much news. I wish there was. Maybe next time there will be more.

Kiss little Olivia for me and give the others my love.

Pa is always kidding me. Last night a man knocked on the back door and I jumped and Pa almost laughed his head off. Just then he was sitting on the couch and asking me if I stayed awake all night, waiting for that man to knock again. He said when Buddy comes home, I'll probably run when he walks in. Just let him come!!

Must close—write soon.

> Lots & Lots of Love,
> Your Sis,
> Annelle

§

July 15, 1944
[Written on Annelle Frees stationery]

Friday

Dearest Mother & All,

I just received your's and Doris' letters and thank you so much. I enjoy getting letters from you.

I do hope you're all well and not working too hard. I know you have plenty to do. I think everything has gone wrong for us. I was just laid off work and now they're not hiring too many people. They're trying to get all the girls into the Army or Navy. Another thing, Mom is sick—She gets worse every day. The doctor told her to get away from the beach at once and to find an apartment is almost impossible. So it goes. I think with everything—I'll go "nuts." I could have gotten a job as riveter in a defense plant, working ten hours a day for $30 a week, but Mom didn't want me to take it. It's twelve miles from here and she says the hours are too long—but I can't find [anything] else. I have to have my birth certificate to get anything now—maybe something will come up. I hope so for I don't have any money to throw away.

I sure [am] glad you got a letter from Buddy. I had three Monday, but haven't heard since. I know he's lonesome for us, but he can't be any more so than I am. I have to write him cheerful letters and believe me, it's plenty hard to do that now. I ask him what he thought of me going into the Navy. I know he won't want me to, but Mom thinks it's just the thing—so to please her I asked him. I'm not old enough yet, though.

I know you're tired of hearing my troubles, so I'll close now. Don't worry, just take care of yourself and write when you can.

Give everyone my love and tell them I think of them always.

> *Lots & Lots of Love,*
> *Annelle*

§

July 4, 1944
[Written on Annelle Frees stationery]

Tuesday, July 4th

My Dearest little Sister,

At last I'm answering your sweet letters I've received. I hope you'll forgive me for not written [sic] sooner. Honestly, Honey, I've just been going around in circles. I know you're always busy.

Today being a holiday, there are thousands of people on the beach. As far as I'm concerned, they can have it. Since I got burned, I don't care too much for it. People just walk all over you, anyway. A little boy hit me on the head with a stick, but I'm still living—Ha!!

How are Mother and the others? Kiss them all for me and give them my love. I'd sure like to see all of you.

So you've been going around quite a bit?!! I'm sure glad you have. I know you had a nice time.

I had a letter from my little husband yesterday. Bless his heart, he's so sweet to write. I do enjoy hearing from him. I miss him very much and pray for him to return safely.

There just isn't any news. I wish there was. I'd like to know something new myself.

The weather is pretty again. Last week was terrible.

Write me as often as you can.
Must close.
> *Lots of love,*
> *your sis*

§

July 6, 1944
[Written on Annelle Frees stationery]

Monday
My Dearest Mother & All,

I received yours and Doris' letters this morning and was so happy to hear from you again and to know you're well. That makes me very happy.

Mother, after I sent the dress, I was afraid you'd think as you did, but please believe me, I wasn't even thinking of that when I bought it. I just liked it and knew you could use it. I think the little pinafore will be cute on Olivia. She's a doll, anyway. I'd give anything to see her—in fact, I'd give anything to see all of you.

I had a letter from Buddy today. It was dated June 18th. He's still fine and said nothing new has happened. Rose sent him a big box of candy and cookies. I hope he gets them. In the news today they said the rocket bombs sent over by the Germans killed quite a few American soldiers in Southern England. I just pray that he is safe and will be home soon and safe.

Betty stayed over Saturday night with me and we lay on the beach Sunday. Today I can hardly sit, I'm burned black. I'll never lie on the beach again. Buddy did the same thing when he was small.

Mom's feeling better and I'm so happy. Pa and I have been keeping house. Pa has decided he wants to visit Daddy on the farm. He's asked about a million questions about farming. He's so anxious to get on a farm. He likes to be on the outside. He wants to see peanuts growing. At first he thought I was kidding about peanuts growing beneath the ground.

That's about all the news. Give my love to Daddy, Joe, Jimmie, Doris, Annette, Olivia and you.

Write everytime you can.
> *Lots & Lots of Love,*
> *Annelle*

§

July 8, 1944
[Written on Annelle Frees stationery]

Saturday, July 8th

My Dearest Mother,

I received your sweet letter today and thank you so much. Your letters are just like a refreshing drink. They give me a new inspiration. Please forgive me for writing what I did in the last letter. I don't know what came over me. I feel much better today and I may go to work Monday in a Drug Co. for $27.50. That helps my feelings, too.

You don't have to worry about me joining the "Waves." Buddy doesn't want me to, either. I was just undecided—now I know.

Mom is better now and I'm so glad. She still doesn't feel too good. Don't think she couldn't get used to a farm. As you know she was born in a small town (Bataan) in Poland. She can get by on anything.

My back is o.k. now—it's started peeling and itches, but feels good.

Kiss little Olivia for me and ask her to write me. Tell Annette and Doris I'd like to hear from them. Give my love to Daddy and the boys. I'd sure like to see all of you.

I just wrote my daily letter to Buddy. I feel rather silly, writing the same thing every day but he looks forward so much that I just can't let him down. He's going through so much for me and still he writes. The least I can do is to keep letters on their way to him. I pray every night for him. He is so good and wonderful.

I'd sure like to be in on that fried chicken. I know it's wonderful. We have chicken every week, but it's boiled or baked, never fried. Mom is a very good cook, though and although most of her dishes are new to me, they're very good.

"Mummy" that's about all for this time. Let me hear from you every time you can, I enjoy hearing from you so much.

> *Lots & Lots of Love,*
> *your Sis,*
> *Annelle*

§

July 16, 1944
[Written on Annelle Frees stationery]

Sunday, July 16th

My Dearest Mother,

I received your very sweet and much appreciated letter yesterday. You'll never know how much I enjoy your letters.

I started to work yesterday at Henshey's, the largest department store in Santa Monica. It's a very nice place to work. They don't pay but $24 plus a small bonus every month. I work in the Sportswear department from 9:30 – 5:30.

We had a letter from Rose today and they were fine. She had a letter from Buddy and he was fine. I didn't have but one letter from him this last week. Bless his heart. I suppose he's busy.

So Dan was home—I know his Mother and Daddy were so happy to see him. I know he looked nice. I'm so glad you and Daddy went to Florida. I know you had a nice time. Yes, Edna wrote me that Doris was in Slocomb. I know she's having a wonderful time. Mom, Pa and I have decided that as soon as Buddy gets home, we're going by car to get you and Daddy and go to Florida for a vacation. Would you like to go? Pa is dying to get out to see Daddy's farm.

The weather is beautiful here now for the first time this week. I heard over the radio that there is a storming on the Carolina coast—I hope it doesn't get to you.

Kiss little Olivia for me and give the others my love. I'd sure like to see all of you.

Mom just went out to take a walk and Pa is listening to the radio.

Mannie's girlfriend is coming out from Chicago next week. They may get married. I hope they do—it would make a different person out of him.

That's all the news for this time. Write every time you can. I'll do the same.

Lots & Lots of Love,

your Sis

§

July 23, 1944
[Written on Annelle Frees stationery]

Sunday
July 23rd
My Dearest Mother,

I received your very sweet letter and thank you so much. I also enjoy hearing from you.

I've been so worried for the past few days. I had a letter—in fact two letters from Buddy Friday and he is in France. Right in the thick of the fighting. The only thing I can do is to pray for his safety and I do every night with all my heart.

Betty stayed with me last night. It was so good to see her again. We lay on the beach today—I'm really a good tan.

Mom's feeling better these days since the news is so good. I only pray that it will continue to be so.

Kiss little Olivia for me and give the others my love.

Mother, I'm sending almost five yards of a beautiful piece of veil material. I found it for only $.49 a yard and bought all she had. It's for you to make you and maybe Annette or Olivia a dress. Just as soon as I have time, I want to get Doris a nice little dress. The ready made are so expensive but they have some beautiful ones where I work.

I'm really enjoying my work. I only pray that I can keep it.

There just doesn't seem to be too much news. Please forgive this short letter. I'll surely do better next time.

Write everytime you can—I love to hear from you.

> *Lots & Lots of Love,*
> *Your Sis,*
> *Annelle*

§

July 24, 1944
[Written on Annelle Frees stationary]

Monday
My Sweet Little "Mummy,"

I received your letter today and believe me, I was so happy to hear from you again. I enjoy your letters so much. They're just as refreshing as a nice rain.

I haven't heard from Buddy since Friday when he told me about him being in France. I've worried so much about him. I only pray that it won't be long before he'll be back. I miss him so much. He's the best husband a woman ever had.

I had a letter from Edna today. She's so sweet to write. She's fine so far and I do hope she continues to be so.

Mom is fine now. I hope she will be well now.

Did you realize that tomorrow week is our first year anniversary. In a way I can hardly realize it.

I think you're having your share of the company. I'm glad that Uncle Charlie could come to visit you. I know all of you laugh your heads off at him. I wish I could be there. I miss you so much.

My week is fine. Today I sold $17.50 of merchandise. It's nice, but after a day's work there and washing my clothes and doing different things, I'm rather tired.

There just isn't much news. As usual I'm wishing I knew something.

"Mummy" write everytime you can. I enjoy hearing from you so much.

Give my love to everyone and kiss little Olivia for me.

Goodnight—

> Lots & Lots of Love,
> Annelle

§

July 27, 1944
[Written on Annelle Frees stationery]

Thursday

My Dearest Little Brother,

Are you surprised to hear from your Sis? I hope you'll have time to read this scratchy writing. I just had to write to the sweetest little brother a sister ever had.

What have you two been doing? I hope you haven't been working too hard. I know you have enough to do, but I know you're sweet to help Mother and Daddy. You'll never be sorry for what you're doing to help them. They're so sweet, angels, be sweet to them. You'll never really know how good they are and what they've done for you until you're away from home.

When Buddy gets home, I promise you two that you are coming out to see us. We'll take you to see anything you want to. We'll go fishing in the ocean on a big boat—Then go out to the island and race back with other boats. We'll go to the Pier where all kinds of rides are all the time, just like the fair. We'll see all the movie stars—see all the shows and go to the horse races. Then we'll go to a play at the Biltmore Theatre. We'll eat at Melody Lane where they have the dining room decorated with gold. All the beautiful things you'll see—ride on the street car and see all the huge department stores. We'll play on the beach. We'll ride down Broadway in Los Angeles where there's millions of cars, buses and people. We'll drive down Laurel Canyon into San Fernando Valley—such beautiful scenery—But remember that's only if you're sweet to Mother and Daddy—and Doris, Annette and Olivia. You have a wonderful family—excluding me, of course—Ha! Ha!

I had two letters from Buddy Tuesday—Poor kid, he's so lonesome. I just pray he'll come home safely and very soon.

That's all, little brothers. Be sweet and remember I still think you're the sweetest brother a sis ever had.

Goodnight and please answer me. I'm including stamps to make sure.

> *Lots or Love –*
> *Annelle*

§

July 31, 1944
[Written on Annelle Frees stationery]

Monday

My Dearest Mother,

I received your very sweet and much appreciated letter today. Thank you so much. I always look forward to your letters. They are so sweet. It's almost like talking to you.

I hope all of you are feeling well and not working too hard. We're all well. Mom went to spend the week with her niece. Pa is cooking for us and believe me he's a good one.

I spent Saturday night and Sunday with Dave and Helen. I sure had a nice time. Sunday afternoon we drove to the zoo and saw every kind of animal—lions, elephants, zebra, camel, raccoon, peacocks, rabbits, bear, leopards, ostrich, monkeys, deer, sheep, porcupine, and millions of others. Most of them, I never heard of. Some very queer looking creatures. Then we drove to the observatory—so you can see all Hollywood, Los Angeles and many other surrounding towns. Some of the most beautiful scenery I've ever seen. It's still very cold here—I don't think we'll have any summer. I wear a heavy coat every day to work—which reminds me, forget the birth certificate. I don't need it. They don't ask for it; only in defense work. Thank you so much my little "Mummy" for writing for it.

I haven't heard from Buddy this week—I only trust that he's well.

I got a permanent today and my hair feels so funny. I didn't have but just a wee bit cut, though.

Kiss little Olivia for me and give the others my love. I love all of you and miss you. I only hope it won't be long until we'll be together.

Goodnight to all!!!

> Lots & Lots of Love,
> Your Sis, Annelle

§

August 7, 1944
[Written on Annelle Frees stationery]

Monday

My Dearest "Mummy"—

I received your very sweet letter and thank you so much. You'll never know how much I look forward to hearing from you. I'm glad all are well. I do hope Doris is better now. Tell her I said to hurry and get well so she can write to me.

I got my first letter from Buddy today in two weeks. He is well and I'm thankful for that. Every day I miss him more and more. Sometimes—(like right now) I feel as though I can't go on. There just seems nothing to live for. I suppose I'm too pessimistic, but Mother—it's hard. I work as hard as I can to keep my mind occupied, but there's always time for thinking. I only pray that it won't be much longer. If only God will let it be over and bring him safely home. If only—God help us that are so weak.

I'm glad you liked the dress. It wasn't anything, I wish I could give you everything you need.

I'm glad you have canned as much as you have. It will sure come in nice in the winter. I'm going to send you plenty of fruit and nut mixtures for your Christmas fruit cake as soon as I have time to go get them.

The weather is still cold and foggy. I hope we'll have some pretty days before long.

Mom is feeling better now and I'm sure glad. She's a different person.

I know you were happy to have Aunt Les and the others to see you. I sure would liked to have seen them.

Mother please forgive this short letter. I have to wash my hair and take a bath. It's now 7:30—so write soon. Give my love to everyone.

Goodnight "Mummy"

> *Lots & Lots of Love,*
> *Your Sis.*

§

August 10, 1944

Thursday

My Dearest Mother,

I received your very sweet letter today and as you know—I was so happy to hear from you. Your letters are always so nice and I do enjoy them. I also had a letter from Aunt Les. She told me about spending the day with you and she said she really enjoyed it. I wish I could have been there.

I have had four letters from Buddy this week. The last one dated July 31st. I sure was happy to hear from him, after waiting two weeks. They are right in the thick of the fighting. They were in the battle of St. Lo. Many in his outfit have been seriously wounded and several killed. I live in suspense all the time—waiting, dreading to see day or night come. Always praying, but wondering. May God bless him and keep him from harm. He's so good and tender-hearted. It hurts me to think of him being over there.

Tell Doris that there's nothing I'd rather do than go home for awhile, but I've just gotten started in this work now and I don't feel I can stop—although I may try to get home for Christmas and stay for a couple of weeks.

Pa found a nice flat in Hollywood. We may move there. It's really beautiful there. Oh! well, any place—just so there's room to lay my head at night—it's days—all right—it doesn't sleep.

I can hardly wait to get the pictures. I know they're good. Is Olivia on them? I hope so. She must be half grown now. I'd give anything to see her.

Tell the boys I got their letters and I did appreciate them very much, but just haven't had time to answer—but I am soon.

Give my love to Daddy and tell him I miss him. Kiss Olivia for me and give my love to all.

Goodnight—answer soon.

> *Lots & Lots of Love, your Sis,*
> *Annelle*

August 21, 1944

Monday

My Dearest "Mummy"

I received your very sweet letter today and I was very happy to hear from you. I always look forward to hearing from you. I know you're very busy and understand if I don't hear from you, but I'll write every time I possibly can.

I had a very sweet letter from Buddy today. He doesn't seem to think that it will be much longer now and I only pray to God that it won't be.

I'm still waiting very patiently for the pictures. I can hardly wait to see them, especially little Olivia. I saw a picture in a magazine that was so much like Olivia—it just made me feel so lonesome to see her and hold her sweet little hands. She's so sweet and beautiful.

I think of every one of you every day—I know you're working so hard. If only there was a way that you wouldn't have to work so hard. I do hope you'll be greatly rewarded this year with a big harvest for every one of you surely deserve the best. I know you'll get it.

I still enjoy my work very much. It keeps me busy every minute I'm there—it isn't so easy, but it sure helps me.

Mom gave me some Ex-lax last night and I was only in the bathroom for 1 hr. and 1 half this morning—Did I run all day? It sure did help me though!!

Give my love to everyone. Kiss Olivia for me.

Goodnight "Mummy"—I'll write every time I can.

> *Lots & Lots of Love,*
> *Annelle*

§

August 24, 1944

Thursday

My Dearest Mother,

I received your very sweet letter written the 20th. I'm glad you got the greeting!! "Mummy" never worry about your deserving anything! I only wish I could give you only half the things, the comforts and ease that you are so worthy of.

You ask for Buddy's address—It is—Sgt. Saul H. Frees—39016446—Service Co.—137th Infantry—A.P.O. 35 c/o Postmaster N.Y.—New York! When you have time to write, I wish you would—He is so busy he might not have to answer for awhile. He would appreciate it very much. He's been in quite a few battles—He still writes though. I had three letters this week. He is so sweet and good!!

I know Olivia is so sweet and beautiful! I'd give anything to see her. I can just see her lying beside Daddy and hear her asking what you're doing? She's just a great, big beautiful doll!

I am always so happy to see a day pass—for I know that it brings the end of the war closer. If only I can keep up. Mom and Pa are really wonderful to me, but I have found that no one can take the place of my own family and Buddy.

I know you dread to see school start. It's such a job. If there is any way I can help, please let me know. I thought for Annette's birthday, I'd give her some underwear and socks for school. All along I'll send a few things to help. I wish I could send everything I'd like to. They have so many cute school clothes. I'll send the boys some socks and shirts. Maybe what I can send will help a little.

I will get the fruit cake materials about Thanksgiving—I can't get them mixed now, but was told I can later. So don't worry yourself about anything nor any money—because I owe you more than I can ever pay.

Be good. God bless you all and give my love to everyone.

> *Lots & Lots of Love,*
> *Always your daughter,*
> *Annelle*

§

August 14, 1944

Monday

My Dearest Mother,

I received your very sweet letter today and you'll never know how happy I was to hear from you again and to know that you're all well. I am well and enjoy my work because it passes away time so fast. That's the main thing. It also enables me to buy bonds. Today I bought a $100.00 bond today. I hope I can keep it up for we'll need it after the war.

I had a very sweet letter from Buddy today—It was written Aug. 4th. It only takes ten days for a letter to get here. They mean so much. He's so sweet to write.

Mother, nothing would make me happier than for you to buy that place. Not that it's such a wonderful place, but at least you'll have something to call home and I know you can make a very nice and comfortable home there.

Yes Mother, I know now that life is not a flowery bed of roses and that you have to make the best of everything. It is hard sometimes, but we have to look up and push forward. There was a time that I thought that you looked for something to worry about, but now I understand what you meant when you said, "Honey, it just comes to me to worry about!" I know that I must have faith. May he look down and guide me for I'm very week—

I know it's early to think of getting materials for a fruit cake, but I thought I'd tell you so you wouldn't go out and worry about getting them when it's so easy for me to do so.

The weather is so beautiful. It's beginning to get hot, but at night it's cool so you can sleep.

I do hope the weather will be nice for awhile so they can get through picking cotton very soon. I think of them so often, knowing it is hot hot and you having so much to do. You have all worked hard, very hard and I know there's something good for all of you.

Mother, I'm rather tired, please excuse this short letter. I send my love to everyone. Kiss little Olivia for me—I'm still waiting for the picture. Answer soon—

> Lots & Lots of Love,
> Your daughter,
> Annelle

§

August 28, 1944

Monday
My Dearest Mother,

I received your very sweet letter today and thank you so much. I always enjoy hearing from you. I'm so sorry that little Olivia isn't feeling well. I hope she is much better now. I'd give anything to see her. I know she's half grown.

Betty came over Saturday afternoon and stayed overnight. We went out for dinner and had Chinese food, came home and both were sick from it. We went to a show Sunday and saw "The Angels Sing!" It wasn't so good, but it passed away time.

Mother, if you can't read my writing in this letter—I'm rather upset—I had a letter from Buddy today. He is in England again in the hospital with a broken ankle. I only hope and pray that he will be all right. Poor kid, he's gone through something terrible. Maybe soon, it will be over. He thinks he will be in the hospital for a month or longer.

I'm glad you could use the olyps [?]. If only I could give you everything you deserve.

Mother, please forgive this short letter, I'm rather tired now. I've been writing letters since 6:30 and it's 7:30—

Goodnight "Mummy." Give my love to everyone. I love every one of you.

Lots & Lots & Lots of Love—
Your Sis, Annelle

§

August 30, 1944

Wednesday
My Dearest Little Sister,

I received your's and Mother's very sweet and much appreciated letters. You can never know how much they mean to me. They are always so nice. I appreciate them even more, knowing that you're so very busy and still take time to write me. Thank you again darling, for writing.

I had another letter from Buddy yesterday. Bless his heart, he's in the hospital in England with a broken ankle. He said in his letter yesterday that he is being moved to a new hospital. I only pray that he will be all right. He's been through so much.

I suppose Edna wrote you about Thallie leaving her. Poor kid, I feel so sorry for her and she's going to have her baby in Sept. Thallie sure should have the seat of his pants kicked. The little "Nut"!!

Tell Mother I am sending Annette a little birthday gift, but don't tell Annette, I'd like to surprise her. If it doesn't fit, send it back and I'll exchange it since I got it at the store.

I was sure surprised to hear about Alvin. Isn't it terrific? I never thought his mother would have such a kid, did you?

The weather here is very nice, but I still have to wear a coat to work every morning.

Darling, I know you're working hard and believe me I think of you every day. You'll be rewarded—just wait.

[Last page missing.]

September 3, 1944

Sunday

My Dearest Mother,

I received your very sweet letter yesterday and as always, I was very happy to hear from you. I hope everyone is well and not too rushed with work, although I know that you have your hands full.

Pa and I went to the show last night. Mom is visiting her cousin and Mannie went out so we decided we didn't have to stay home.

Yes Mother, your letters have air mail stamps on them. I don't know if it takes longer for your letters to come here, but I don't think it does.

I'm by myself right now. Pa went out for a walk—so I cleaned the house, took a bath, shampooed and rolled my hair. I don't have to work tomorrow since it's Labor Day so I intend to get the rest of my work done.

I had several letters from Buddy this week. He is beginning to be able to use crutches—just for a minute or two at a time. I only hope that the doctor set his ankle right so he doesn't limp.

Well, the war news is sounding good, but now—of all times, we must work just twice as hard now so we can finish it off before many weeks have passed. A reporter is giving the latest news now and the boys seem to be about twelve miles from Germany!! I heard that Hitler (the rat) didn't give his stinking speech. He better keep his trap shut, but tight!!

Did I tell you that Charles wrote Betty that he slept on a German land mine all night? Is he lucky?

Kiss little Olivia for me. Give Daddy, the boys, Doris and Annette my love and kiss them for me.

Write to me every time you can and I understand when I don't hear from you.

Lots & Lots of Love,
Annelle

§

September 8, 1944

Friday

My Dearest Mother,

I received your very sweet letter and the pictures. They were so very good and thank you. Little Olivia is becoming more beautiful every day. I'd sure give anything to see her. In the one with you and Olivia, you have your head down and she is looking sideways and I can't see your faces, but the other with Daddy and Annette with you and Olivia is exactly like every one of you and it's very good. Where were Doris and the boys? I'd sure like to have had one of them.

I sure hope Frances will be all right and I know she will be. How do she and Harold get along? I hope nicely.

I had four letters from Buddy this week. He seems to be fine. They took his leg out of one cast and put it in another. He's very lonesome—you know he has so much time to think—but does some sketching and reads quite a bit. He hasn't had a letter from me in about six weeks since he's been moving so often, but I don't think it will be too long now.

I know Daddy and the children are having such a time and believe me I think of them so much. It's just getting warm here—was rather hot today—I didn't even have to wear a coat.

My work is all right, but I was rather tired today. Mrs. Brenton, our buyer is giving me another responsibility—dressing the windows and I'm doing a little modeling. It's really fun and I enjoy it—It passed the time much faster.

"Mummy," I must say goodnight now. Be sweet and give my love to everyone. I love every one of you.

> *Lots & Lots of Love,*
> *Annelle*

§

September 11, 1944

Monday

My Dearest Mother,

I received your very sweet letter today and thank you very much!! I also received two letters from Buddy also. They were very sweet, as they are always. He is all right, but I can't understand though why they keep changing the cast on his leg. This is the third time. I only hope they know what they are doing. I bought his Christmas presents Saturday. It's so hard to buy things that you can send and that he can use. I bought tooth brush, tooth paste, shave cream, razor blades, books, candy, stationary and soap—and deodorant.

I am so glad that little Annette liked her slip. Today is her birthday—will you tell her that I would like to wish her a very happy birthday. Kiss her for me.

I think of you and the others working so hard, I just wish I could find some way for you to have more time to just rest.

Mother, it's true—I can't do half as much as far as getting things for the children, but please tell me what color sweaters that Doris, Annette and the boys could use better with the things they have. I can get all wool sweaters for about eight dollars—and I want to do that much. We have some very nice ones. Oh! if only I had the money, I could get them so many beautiful clothes. But it is terrible the prices they put on things. You know cotton dresses can't be bought for less than $10.00. It hurts me to see how selfish and greedy some people are—and the worst part is the more they have, the more they want—But they all have to grumble about something. Sometimes I wonder what we are headed for.

Mother, I think you should have some nice fat chickens about Christmas—who knows—maybe Buddy and I will be there to help eat some.

Give my love to Daddy and the children.

Betty and I had a nice week-end. We saw "Dragon Seed"—a very good picture.

I must say good night now. Write every time you can and so will I.

> Lots & Lots of Love,
> Annelle

§

September 17, 1944

Sunday

My Dearest Mother,

I received two letters from you yesterday and believe me I was very happy to hear from you. One letter had an air mail stamp and one didn't. Do you need some stamps "Mummy"? If so, please tell me and I'll send you some.

Oh! I know you dread school, but if they are out at one, it isn't quite so bad. I do hope the crop comes out good. All of you have worked so hard and I've thought of you so often. I only wish I could do something to relieve you of the strain.

I had a card from Mary Lou Fussell yesterday. She and Leslie are in Santa Maria about 400 miles from here. I wish Les could get a few days off and they could come out—I'd give anything to see them. I imagine he must be going overseas soon. I hope not.

Poor little Buddy is doing very well. He says—"I'm doing something for the war effort, rolling bandages—I say there's nothing too good for our boys." I had to cry when I read it for only God knows what he has been through. He never did tell me how he broke his ankle. I just hope they'll send him home very soon.

Rose sent me a box of the nicest things—slips pajamas, dresses, gowns, housecoats and a good compact. Everything fits perfectly.

Gee! but this is a dreary Sunday. Nothing to do—Mom and Pa are sleeping and I'm just plain miserable. Oh! well if that's all I have to worry about, I'm fine.

"Mummy" dear I must close now. Give my love to Daddy, Doris, Joe, Jimmie, Annette and Olivia. Kiss them for me.

Write when you can.

> Lots & Lots of Love,
> Your daughter,
> Annelle

§

September 21, 1944

Thursday
Mother, Darling—

If you can't read this letter, please forgive me but I have such a terrific stomach ache, I can hardly see. As a matter of fact I couldn't write a long letter to Buddy. I just took a Midol tablet—sure hope it relieves me.

I received yours and Joe's very sweet letters. I was so happy to hear from you again. I do hope all of you are well.

Mother, you'll never know how happy I am that Daddy has gotten as much done toward buying that place as he has. I sure think he is wise. He is a good manager when he has a chance. I don't think I'll ever forget how he used to buy and sell mules and cows. It shows he is thrifty and believe me one can make profit on such now. I only pray you can get a new house and get running water and lights. I've prayed that someday you would have a home of your own for no other deserves it more than you. I kind of felt "down in the dumps" today and you'll never know how good it made me feel to get your letter and hear that you've at least gotten this far. It will mean so much after the war. Believe me, everyone is going to be begging for some place to live and work. I can't say it's such a wonderful location, but it could be made a wonderful place. After seeing so many silly, wild and greedy people, I think the country is the best. Here, no one thinks of anything but money, beautiful clothes and some place to go. Thank God, I can be happy at home.

It's getting cool here and oh, it's beautiful. I'd give anything if you could see the big, blue waves coming in on the beach. Oh! but it is beautiful.

Joe, Darling, I'm going in to the men's department and see about the shirt. I don't know exactly what you're talking about, but I can get some nice ones for you and Jimmie. I'll have to take a few things at a time, but just wait Darling, I'll get to everyone. Mother, I didn't forget about your favorite fruitcake materials—Just thought I'd wait until you're ready to make it. I want to get enough to make a big one in your cooker. Gee! I think I'll have to go home to help eat it.

I had two letters from Buddy this week. He hasn't heard from me in about 6 weeks. I hope he hears soon. He is able to walk around now with the aid of a crutch.

Kiss little Olivia for me. Give my love to Doris, Annette, Joe, Jimmie and my Daddy and "Mummy." I'd sure like to see you.

I'm knitting some little things for Edna's and Frances' babies. Goodness—they better take their time or I can't keep up making things for all the new ones.

Thank Heaven, since Rose sent me all those things I won't have to buy anything now for a long, long time. Thanks to her.

Every night I listen to the news—I only hope we can finish this job very soon.

Mother Darling, I have to close now, although I feel so much better than I did when I started this—I just ran out of news.

Write every time you can. Let me know all the new developments. Sure glad you had the peanuts poisoned—It may save you four times the cost.

Kiss everyone for me and give them my love.

Goodnight "Mummy"—I love all of you—

Your Sis,
Annelle

§

September 27, 1944

Wed.

Mother, Darling,

I received your very sweet letter yesterday and as you, I was more than glad to hear from you. I do hope that Doris and Jimmie feel much better and that everyone is well.

We are well—I have a sore finger and can't write very well, but it doesn't hurt—just got a splinter in it. I feel fine otherwise.

I had a letter from Buddy Monday—He said he would probably see Tokio before California. It didn't sound too good. As you know everyone seems to think the Germans will hold out until next Spring—I only hope and pray that they don't. It's rather heart-breaking—everything is turned around and seems strange—If it would help—I'd sit down and cry, but I know it wouldn't help. We have to ask God to guide us and protect us through the dark and dangerous days.

Joe, Darling—I'm sending you a shirt. I hope you like it—you can tell the boys you're wearing an expensive one, too. I think it looks just like you. I will see about Jimmie's next week—I'll take it one at a time and I think it will be better.

Mother, there just doesn't seem to be any news and my hand is rather tired, so I'll close. Let me know all the news. Give my love to Daddy, Doris, Joe, Jimmie, Annette and Olivia.

> *Lots & Lots of Love,*
> *Annelle*

P.S. I am going to see about Annette's little scissors tomorrow!!

§

October 2, 1944

Monday

Mother, Darling,

I received your very sweet letter today and as you know, I was very glad to hear from you. You're so wonderful to write and I appreciate every letter more and more, knowing that you have so much to do and yet find time to write to one. I do have the most wonderful family!

I had a letter from Buddy today! Bless his heart—he's so faithful to write. He hasn't had but one letter from me in two months and I write every night. Somehow the letter I got from him today was almost too much for me. He told me that there are so many ugly and cruel pictures of war in his mind and it's so hard to try to forget them. He began by saying—"Darling, I didn't get a letter from you today, but that is all right. I read your last one"—(which made 50 times). Then he thinks I'm wonderful because I write and I'm true to him. Mother, I know that he is the most wonderful husband any girl ever had. I only pray for God to guide him and bring him safely home.

I know Olivia is beautiful and I'd give anything to see her. As a matter of fact, I'd sure like to see all of you. Mother, I won't promise I'll be home for Xmas. I'll try—but I thought maybe Buddy would be home but from the way he talks, he may be gone for a couple of years yet. I may be able to get home. So much is involved—it costs quite a bit and I would have to give up my job because when I go, I'll go for a couple of months.

Mother, I know you have so many things to do and to worry you and maybe I shouldn't say this, but sometimes I wonder what's in store for us. Will the war ever be over!! If only we could live a normal life. Maybe I'm a pessimist, but it's rather hard, wondering, waiting, praying and hoping!

Kiss little Olivia for me and give everyone my love.

I finished Edna's baby's soakers and now I'm knitting Annette a sweater. It will probably be a long time before I finish it. I must start Frances' baby a pair of soakers very soon.

Mother, forgive this short letter—I'll write again soon.

> *Lots & Lots of Love,*
> *your loving daughter,*
> *Annelle*

§

October 8, 1944

Sunday

Mother, Darling,

I received your very sweet letter and the clipping yesterday—Thank you so much for both. I enjoy your letters so very much. I do hope all of you are well. I know you are so busy that you can't see though. I think of you so often, knowing you have so much to do. I only wish I could help you.

We are all well!! I'm still working. I enjoy it, but I'm so lonesome for Buddy and of course my own family. Buddy writes often. I've had two letters this week. Bless his heart, he is so faithful. The last two letters I got were long. He is so lonesome and every letter he writes, I can't help crying. He said in his last letter that he felt silly when he felt sorry for himself because he thought I got the worse deal, being in new surroundings and having to act and live as usual. He is so good and sweet. I would give anything to see him.

Betty came over last night. We went out for dinner and then to a show. We did some Christmas shopping. I bought part of Olivia's things. I'm taking it one at a time. There's not too much to choose from, but I'm getting quite a few things—just little things—Something they can use.

I sent Buddy's Christmas present a couple of weeks ago. I wish I knew that he could be home for Christmas!!

Mother, how do you feel these days? I hope you aren't having any headaches like you used to.

Mother, I'll try to get home for Christmas, but I don't know. It would cost me about $150 for round trip and too I would have to give up my job. You see, there are so many things involved. I'm saving as much money as I can, but Gee! it takes about ten times as much here to get by. There are always things coming up that I don't expect.

Mother, give my love to daddy, Doris, Joe, Jimmie, Annette and Olivia!! Tell them I miss them all and would like to see every one of you.

> *Lots & Lots of Love,*
> *your daughter,*
> *Annelle*

§

October 14, 1944

Saturday
My Darling Mother,

I received your very sweet letter today and thank you so, so much. You'll never know how I enjoy them. Thank Daddy for saying "hello"—It's been a long time since he said anything to me. When you have time Daddy—write me a few lines.

Yes, I know I must keep my chin up, but so many times, it is rather hard to do!! Like tonight, listening to the radio—no one's here but Mom and me and is it lonesome. It's Saturday night and if I thought it would help—I could sure cry.

I'm so glad you found time to write to Buddy. I write every night, but he doesn't hear from me but about twice a month—I get his letters, but he doesn't get mine. I think I told you his cast is off and he will be going back into action— I only pray for God to watch over him and keep him safe. If only I could know how he has suffered. Bless his heart, he is so sweet to write and he writes the most wonderful letters.

Talking about Annette's sweater, I sure hope she can wear it when I finish it. I have started on the arm holes and I'm sure no good at following my directions on this particular part of the sweater. When I do finish, it should be rather nice. I finished one pair of soakers and must start the others.

Did I tell you that Betty's husband, Charles, is in a French hospital? He has some kind of infection, not too serious. Poor kid, she's so worried. Believe me she is a wonderful girl—She's been so good to me and from the first time Mom saw her, she liked her very much.

Gee! we were so, so busy at the store today. I had $163.00 on my book and that isn't bad. They must take in about three or four thousand a day—not bad for a medium size dept. store.

Well, I put $75 in the bank this week which brings our account up to $135 in the bank and $200 in bonds. I have to stretch every penny to do it, but I get it there. I don't like to have to spend my allotment checks if I can get by otherwise.

Kiss little Olivia for me—Give everyone my love and kiss yourself for me.

Lots & Lots of Love,
Your Sis,
Annelle

§

October 20, 1944

Friday
My Dearest Mother,

I received your very sweet letter from—you didn't date it!!—It just says Tues. A.M. I am so glad that all of you are well. I am well and not working so hard right now.

I know that you have so many things to keep you busy and unable to answer my letters on time, so I try to understand!!

I just can't imagine Aunt Flora expecting!! Gee! I'm so happy for her and I know she is, too. Well, she should, while she's young and can enjoy them. I'm sure glad Edna came through fine and I'm glad she has a boy—It's a very sweet name!! I just haven't had time to send the soakers—I finished them, but I'm forever running, doing something—but I must get them in the mail.

Tell little Annette that I appreciated her letter very much. It was so sweet of her to write. I would write her separate, but I have quite a few things to do.

Mother, don't worry about me stinting myself. The reason I started shopping so early is so I can buy a little every week and then I can manage nicely. You see, Mother, every month I get 3% of all over $50 I bring in daily. This month I got $19.96—so it's just like finding that! For Christmas, I will get 5% of all over $50 daily I've brought in since I'm there, which should run pretty close to $50. I don't think it's too bad—If I gave it up to go home, I'd lose the Christmas present. So I think I'll go the first of the year. It will give me a chance to save enough money to go and then I won't have to take any out of the bank.

Well, "Mummy," that's about all. Give everyone my love and write every time you can.

Lots & Lots of Love, Your Sis, Annelle

P.S. I found some of the cutest things for Annette and Olivia—for Christmas.

§

October 30, 1944

Monday

Mother, Darling,

I received yours and Doris' very sweet letters today. Thank you both so much for them. It was from Oct. 28th. You can never know how much I appreciate them.

Mother, I know you have so much to do. I think of you so, so much. I am so glad though that the crop is as near gathered as it is. I know you are, too.

Well, I had another letter from Buddy today. He is still in the hospital. He finally got all my letters. He got 65 at once. Bless his heart, he was so happy to get them.

"Mummy," how would you like for me to come home about Xmas Eve or Christmas Day? If I can make my reservation on the plane, I'll fly in—if not, I'll go by train. If I can get to go by plane, I'll get to be home for Xmas—If not, it will be a few days afterwards!! At any rate, I'll be there about that time. I'm already getting excited. Gee! I hope I can fly. It cost the same by plane as by Pullman and they take care of everything. It only takes about 18 hours to fly, but 74 by train.

My job is still fine. The girls are very nice, but—I'd still rather see all of you.

"Mummy," I'm tired and I have some ironing to do, so I must say goodnight now. Give my love to Daddy, Doris, Joe, Jimmie, Annette and Olivia.

> *Lots & Lots of Love,*
> *Annelle*

§

November 3, 1944

Friday

My Darling "Mummy,"

I received your very sweet letter from Oct. 30. I was sure glad to hear from you! Your letters are almost like being there and talking to you. I can see you sitting there, writing and it makes me so lonesome to see you.

I know you are so busy. I can see you rushing around in the morning to get your work done and I'm there, trying in my stupid way to help. Well, it won't be too long now. I wanted to get there in time for Christmas, but my buyer almost had fits when I told her. She wants me to stay until the first because of the rush, so I'll have to wait until then. At any rate, I'll be there. Yes, I've talked it over with Mom and Pa. Mom says she doesn't blame me at all. I wrote Buddy, but I didn't get an answer yet. I'm sure he won't mind, but be happy. I'd give anything to be there and see the kids when they open their packages. Oh! I got some of the cutest things—I would love to have them to play with. For Doris and the boys—and you and Daddy—I didn't get any toys!! I couldn't resist for Annette and Olivia. I also found a cute thing for Jimmie!!

Mother, I'll send the cake materials next week. I think it's a good idea for you to make your cake early.

I got a letter from Mary (Fussell) Bavkert today. She is fine and sends her love.

We're expecting Rose and Marie. Mom is so excited. I don't know when they'll be here. Did I tell you that Buddy got 65 letters from me? Bless his heart, he was so happy!! I had four from him this week, all very sweet.

"Mummy," give my love to Daddy, Doris, Joe, Jimmie, Annette and Olivia. I'll be flying in soon after Christmas, so be looking for me.

> *Lots & Lots of Love,*
> *Your Sis,*
> *Annelle*

November 13, 1944
[Written on Henshey's Dept. Store stationery]

Monday

Mother, Darling,

I received your very sweet letter today and as you know, I was so happy to hear from you. I do hope all of you are well and not working too hard.

I am well—I can't say I'm too happy—but I'll never be until Buddy is home. I had two letters from him. Mother, I knew that war does things to people—It has to Buddy. His letters are still wonderful, sweet and loving, but I know by some of the things he's tried to tell me. There are so many horrible pictures in his mind. If only I could help him. He is so wonderful, but for the first time—he is so alone and miserable—I love him so much, but I'm helpless.

Mother, it seems as though I can't get together on my plans. Now, I suppose it will be after Xmas before I get home. Since there are so many planes crashing up—I think I may take the train. I have to work until Xmas for the 5%.

Mother, I'll have to send the Xmas gifts before the 1st, but don't let the kids open them. Don't let the boxes scare you, it's just that the toys take up quite a bit of space. I sent the cake materials last week. I hope you got them.

Well, tomorrow I'll be twenty—getting old.

Must close—write every time you can. Give everyone my love.

> *Always your loving daughter,*
> *Annelle*

§

November 16, 1944

Wednesday

My Darling Mother,

I received your very sweet letter from Nov. 12th. It was very sweet and as you know I was more than glad to get it.

I hope all of you are well and not working too hard. I'm fine, but rather busy. I hardly have time for anything.

Last night Mom and I went to the show and saw I Love a Soldier!! It was very good, but sad. I cried all through it. Tomorrow night the girls at the store are taking me to China Town in L.A. for dinner. Tuesday was my birthday, but we couldn't go then. Betty bought something for me, but said she'd bring it over.

Dave and Helen are taking me out Saturday. Everyone is wonderful to me, but none can take Buddy's place. On my last birthday I said goodbye to him when he went to Tenn. and this year he's overseas. I only pray that God should bless him. I hear from him about three times a week. He says he doesn't write as often as he should, but something gets hold of him and he just can't.

Did you get the cake materials? I do hope you did.

Mother, please don't worry about my check. I can't have it changed because I don't have my application number since I lost my card. I didn't ask Nadine why she didn't write. If she doesn't want to be bothered, I'll give her the money for postage.

I know little Olivia has grown. I can hardly wait to see her as well as the others. I had a letter from Mary Lou today and she may go back with me, I hope she does.

I had a letter from Aunt Les. She said Uncle Terry is moving to Atlanta.

I'm tired. Mother—I've written three letters and it was 12:00 last night when I got to bed.

Give my love to everyone. Kiss you for me.

> *Lots & Lots of Love,*
> *Annelle*

§

November 19, 1944

Sunday

Mother, Darling,

How are you tonight? I do hope you are well and happy!!

If you would like to know how I am, I'll tell you. I had a telegram from Buddy—He is in New York and may be here any day. I talked to him today on the phone. He sounded wonderful. I was so excited I cried and shook all over and I still am. He sounded so wonderful. We talked about 8 or 9 minutes!! Mother, I can hardly wait. He's so wonderful. May God bless him. I prayed every night. I know prayers are answered if they are in earnest.

I will send you a telegram as soon as he gets here so don't be alarmed when you get it.

Kiss little Olivia for me and give everyone my love.

I can never tell you how happy I am.

When we were talking he said, "Baby, when I get hold of you, I'll never let you go." He said I missed you so much!!

I must close now. I'm still very excited. I'll write again soon.

> *Lots & Lots & Lots of Love,*
> *Your Sis,*
> *Annelle*

§

November 25, 1944

Saturday

My Dearest Mother,

I received your very sweet and much appreciated letter. I was beginning to get a wee bit worried. I do hope all of you are well and have not too much work to do.

You must have gotten my letter by now, telling you that Buddy is in New York. Mother, you can never know how happy I am. I got two letters from him this week. They were very sweet. He is so very happy to be back. He thinks he may be sent to San Francisco. Oh! I can hardly wait. He may get a furlough, I hope.

Mother, I'm sure glad you got the cake materials, but so sorry the package was torn. That's all I sent. As a matter of fact, it was all I could get. I only hope you can use it.

Mother, is it O.K. if I send the Christmas gifts next week? I want them to get there on time and they tell us to mail them by the first. If they should get there early—maybe you can hide them.

I have so many things to do now before Buddy gets home so I don't have to do anything when he gets here.

I had a letter from Mary yesterday. She thinks Leslie may have to leave soon. Poor kid, I feel so sorry for her—I can only imagine how she feels. I know you must have been sick after the tests, but it's a good idea to have it done.

Please kiss little Olivia for me and give Daddy, Doris, Joe, Jimmie and Annette my love and kiss you for me.

Goodnight "Mummy"—I'll write again soon. I love all of you!!!

> *Your loving Sis,*
> *Annelle*

§

November 30, 1944

Thursday

Mother, Darling,

I received your very sweet letter today. I was so happy to hear from you again. I do hope all of you are well. I know you are so very busy, but I suppose everything is about done as far as harvesting is concerned and you can know that I am so thankful. I know it will take a load off your shoulder. There's never a minute I don't think of you, knowing you're working so hard. If only I could make it easier for you.

Yes Mother, it is so wonderful to know Buddy is back. I also had to pinch myself to see if I was dreaming. I think I told you about talking to him on the phone. Oh! he sounded so wonderful. I can hardly wait to see him. I only pray for God to bless him and keep him. I've been getting one or two letters every day from him until today. He wrote a very sweet letter on Thanksgiving Day—He told me he was so thankful to the one who presides over our destinies. Mother, they just don't come any better than he is. He doesn't know when he will get to come here. They are (or may) keep him there for a few weeks, so I can't make any plans at all. He hopes to get home for Christmas, but he doesn't know yet.

I just finished wrapping the kids' Christmas gifts. I only hope they get there O.K. I'm sending them early so they'll get there on time.

Well business is sure getting good. I wouldn't mind having the money we take in every day—you know—in our department alone—we take in about $800 per day.

Mom is so happy she can hardly see. She runs around in circles all the time. Pa is happy, too, but he doesn't show excitement like Mom.

We've been having some beautiful weather for the past few weeks, but it looks as though the rainy season may start in any time now.

Gee! I've been trying to get everything done before Buddy gets here. Believe me, I had plenty to do, too.

How is my darling little Olivia? I'll bet she says everything now. I'd give anything to see her. Give her a big kiss for me. I'll bet little Annette is grown by now. Tell her to write me when she can and I think she might like Santa this year. I suppose Doris is too busy with her dates now to know what's going on. I was kidding, Honey. Give my grown brothers a big kiss for me and tell them I'd sure like to see them. I know they're men now. How is my Daddy? I hope he's well and happy. Tell him I love him and he should write when he has time. Mother Darling, give yourself a great, big kiss and I love you very much. Please don't work too hard. Maybe you'll have two more kids with you before long.

"Mummy," that's about all for now. I've exhausted my weak mind for news. So don't work too hard and write as often as you can.

> *Lots & Lots & Lots of Love,*
> *Your loving daughter,*
> *Annelle*

§

December 4, 1944

Monday

My Darling Mother,

I received your very sweet letter, very sweet letter from Nov. 29th today. I also got the clippings. Gee! It hardly seems possible that Betty's baby has grown so much. It has been a year, but it hardly seems possible. I'm sure glad that Ruby is getting married and I hope she will be very happy.

I had a letter from Mary Lou today. She is under the doctor's care. She worries too much and is on the verge of a nervous breakdown. I feel so very sorry for her, but I think she is doing the wrong thing by taking on so much work and the worries she has—it's too much for anyone.

I had two very wonderful letters from Buddy today. He still doesn't know when or where he'll be going. It will be somewhere in the states. Mother, I think he was sent back because of his ankle, but I can't be sure until he's here for he won't tell me everything—I only pray to God that I can know how to be thankful for his safe return. I can hardly wait until I can see him. I don't know when he will be here. He won't be going overseas anymore. May God be with him and bless him. I love him more than I can ever find words to tell. He's so wonderful.

Gee! I'd sure like to be there, eating chicken and stuff!! I can taste it now. If only Buddy and I could be there to help eat everything!!! Maybe soon we will—I can't make any plans until I know where Buddy will be.

Goodnight "Mummy"—Give everyone my love.

> *Lots & Lots of Love,*
> *Your Sis,*
> *Annelle*

§

December 13, 1944

Wednesday
Mother, Darling,

I received your very sweet letter and you can never know how much they mean to me.

Gee, I think everyone has a new baby. Well, I am happy for them. I'll bet Frances' little baby is cute. I would like to see her. Mother, I'm ashamed—but I have never finished her baby's soakers yet. I've been so very busy. It may seem silly to think I'm busy, but honestly—there is always something to do. By the time I get home from work, Mom has dinner made—I eat and it's already dark and then you know I like to get to bed as early as possible.

I'm so glad you signed the deeds and I pray that everything goes well and very soon the place will be paid for. You surely deserve it, if anyone ever did.

So—Daddy has new mules—That's very good. At least they can stand the ploughing that has to be done.

How is poor little Jimmie? I do hope he is much better. I've thought of him so much. Bless his heart, he hasn't been well for a long time.

How are the kids doing in school? I'm sure they're doing well. I'll bet they can hardly wait until Christmas. I can hardly believe it's so near because the weather is so beautiful. It's just wonderful. We are preparing for it. I just got one, (the big one) package off to you Tuesday. I hope it won't be late getting there.

We start working until 9:00 Saturday. There are two shifts—from 9:30-6:00 and the others work 12:00-9:00. I will take the early shift Saturday. Mr. Henshey told me I could because Buddy will be home Saturday. He is near San Diego. He expects a furlough the last of this week. I only wish they would give him a discharge. Oh! I can hardly wait. I had a telegram from him Tues. morning that he had arrived in Calif. Gee! you should see Mom—is she excited. We bought him some nice gifts. I hope his furlough lasts long enough for us to go out. I have to work all next week since it's the week before Christmas. Friday night the girls are having a party—so I have to attend. We drew names and give small gifts.

Kiss little Olivia and Annette for me. Give Doris, Joe and Jimmie and Daddy my love.

I must close now. I have to write a letter for Mom to a cousin.

Goodnight Mummy. Always your loving daughter,
Annelle

January 6, 1945

Saturday

Mother, Darling,

I'm writing this because I feel as though I haven't written anything since Buddy has been home because we were always going out.

I do hope that all of you are well and not working too hard.

I just got back from the station after seeing Buddy off to the hospital again. The three weeks he was here were perfect. He is so nervous. He screamed at everyone when they said anything. He can't help it, but it just doesn't seem like him. He yelled at Mom so much that she got scared. He was wonderful to me, but still I worry about his condition. I think they will be able to do quite a bit for him at this hospital. They have every kind of recreation so he will be kept busy.

I would give anything if we could have gone home, but I can't begin to give you the reasons why we didn't. First, we wouldn't have had any time to stay— the trains are crowded—Buddy can't stand to ride and of course there's the question of money. He may get a discharge—I only pray that he does and then I'm going and nothing can stop me.

You should see the medals Buddy is wearing! The one on the left is the purple heart, the center one is European theatre of war, the one on the right is a good conduct medal he got before going over. The big one on the bottom is combat infantryman's badge. I think he looks good to have been through what he has. He doesn't limp very much.

How are all of you? What about little Olivia? I wish I could see her. I'll bet she is grown by now. I know the boys are men now. Kiss them for me. How is Annette? Bless her heart, she is so sweet. I hope she likes school. And my grown-up sister, Doris. She must be a beautiful lady. I can hardly wait to see her graduate. Please kiss Daddy for me and tell him when he can write. Kiss yourself for me.

I suppose I didn't have as much to write as I thought I did.

I must close now—I have a few things of Buddy's to wash out. So be good and don't work too hard.

> *Lots & Lots of Love,*
> *Annelle*

§

January 10, 1945

Wednesday
Dearest Mother,

I received your very sweet letter of Jan. 3rd. It was very sweet and thank you so much. Your letters are almost like talking to you.

I am sorry that little Olivia has a cold. I do hope that she is much better now. Give her a big kiss for me. I wish I could hear her talk. Tell me what she says! I know she is more beautiful (if that is possible).

Mother, I know that you are so busy. I only wish I could be there to help you. I am glad you're quilting some for I know that you need it. I hope you can get plenty of them for the winter. (Seems funny to say winter; it isn't cold here).

You must have been surprised to see Miss Mae. I know you enjoyed having them. Did Shirley come? If she did—I'm sure she and Annette had a wonderful time.

I'd sure like to be there, eating fresh meat with you—I can just see those nice ribs and baked potatoes. Oh! how good it would be to grease my fingers with it.

Mother, I'd give anything if Doris could have her teeth fixed. If Aunt Les can help a little—I will also help. I will pay as much as you say—Just let me know. It would make all the difference for she is beautiful and I know she would be happier.

I do hope you get a pump put in. It will be much better and safer.

I had a letter from Buddy today. He is fine. I just finished a letter to him. He is 200 miles from here and will be able to come in rather often.

Goodnight Mother Darling. Give my love to Daddy—Jimmie, Doris, Annette, and Olivia. Always your loving daughter, *Annelle*

§

January 13, 1945

Saturday
Mother Darling,

I received your very sweet letter today. It was from the 7th. It was so good to hear from you again. I do enjoy your letters so very much.

I'm well and do hope all of you are also. Buddy came home Thursday night on a three day pass. He was very sick yesterday and last night, but feels better tonight. I think he has flu. He has a terrible cold and his head and stomach are bothering him. Bless his heart—he just isn't well. His leg is perfectly well. He only limps when it's damp. They sent him back here because of a nervous condition. I don't think he will go back overseas—It might be that he will get out. I do pray that he will. He was in the army three years the 8th of this month. I think he's had enough—He is sitting here beside me, talking to Mom and Pa—about the things he did when he was a little boy.

Thank you for sending Olivia's kiss to me. I only wish I could see her and really kiss her. Buddy hasn't said anything about me going home yet—so I don't know what to tell you. If he does, you won't have to worry—I'll let you know. I'd give anything if I could, but I can't until he says. We don't know what will be with him yet.

I'm happy you finished the quilt—I only hope you can quilt plenty of them for I know you can use quite a few more.

It's too bad about Joe's Grandmother. I was very sorry to hear about it.

So Ruth Griffin and Auburn were married. That is a surprise. I didn't even know they care about each other.

Gee! they must need men for the army—taking Taylor and Herman from the farm. Is Wilma married yet? If she had a chance she probably is.

How is my Daddy? When he isn't too tired, tell him to please write me a few lines!! Kiss Annette for sending me such a wonderful letter. It was very sweet of her to think to write me.

How are they boys? They must be very busy. They're so sweet to help.

Where is Harold stationed? Poor Frances, left with a baby and him away.

I wish you would send me James Edward's address so I could write him. Does Aunt Mimmie know where he is?

Mother—Goodnight Darling—Don't work too hard and write often.
    Lots of Love,
    Buddy & Annelle

§

January 18, 1945

Thursday
My Dearest Mother,
    I do hope all of you are well and not working too hard. I'm afraid that I don't feel too good. My stomach is bothering—I can't go to the bathroom.

Mother, I'm sending the material for Doris' pajamas—I'm also enclosing a pattern (I didn't know if she has one), buttons and thread. I'm sending a few safety pins I happened to find when I was shopping. I'm sending a few things that I thought Doris might use for around home. They aren't very good, but maybe she can get some good from them and you know how Buddy is about me wearing house dresses. I don't know how good the material is—I was lucky to find it. The piece I wanted to get was $1.29 a yd. and I just couldn't get it.

I had a letter from Mary Bankert (Fussell) and she's going home. Leslie is going overseas. I feel so sorry for her.

Mother—forgive this short letter. I'm rather tired and too I want to take a bath.

Kiss everyone for me and write often.

> *Lots of Love,*
> *Annelle*

§

January 23, 1945

Tuesday

My Dearest Mother,

I received your letter yesterday and as you know I was very glad to hear from you. It is almost like talking to you.

I was so sorry to hear that James Reid is "Missing." I know it's killing his Mother. May God bless her. And to think we have troubles. I do hope that they find he is a prisoner, but I suppose it would be better for him if he wasn't for they torture them so.

Oh! I'm so glad that Henry is home. I can only imagine how excited Thelma is. I would like very much to see him. Will you give him my love!!!

I'm sorry Doris is sick. I do hope she feels much better now. I'm sure they'll give her tests over to her.

Yes, Mother—Buddy has been through so very much. I only pray to God to help me to know how to help him overcome that nervous condition. He tries so hard not to show it, but sometimes he can't hide it. Mother, he wasn't wounded—exactly. During a battle, he ran for his foxhole and stumbled on something and fell. He broke an ankle. They sent him to England to heal that as fast as possible so he could go back into action. While he was there, they noticed how nervous he was and investigated immediately and it wasn't long until he found out he was coming home. The doctor told him he should never have gone overseas. They say no actor should go over because they are all very nervous, anyway.

I know you are so busy. I can just see you, running from daylight until dark. It's just about that way with me, especially with Mom in a rest home. Pa does all the cooking, but I plan the meals, make Mannie's lunch and clean the house. Then I work all day. Yesterday I washed—Buddy had quite a few clothes to do and tonight I have to iron. By the time I do a few things, I like go to bed so I can get up early.

Talking about Doris' teeth—I'm going to do my best to send some money to help you. I may have to wait until I get my monthly bonus—and send it in small portions, but I'll do all I can.

I hope you got the package so Doris can have her material for her pajamas.

How is little Olivia? Oh! I'd give anything to see her. I know she's grown so much.

Oh! did I laugh at Jimmie's letter. It was very cute. Thank him and Annette for their very sweet letters.

Give my love to Daddy, Joe and Doris.

I have three more letters to write—Solly, James Ed. and Pauline Brown. I also have a big ironing to do—so I have to say goodnight for now.

> *Lots & Lots of Love,*
> *Annelle*

§

January 31, 1945

Wednesday

Dearest Mother,

I received your letter today and it was so very good to hear from you again.

I do hope everyone is feeling well and not working too hard. I feel fine. I have a cold, but that's nothing unusual for me. "Mummy" don't worry about the fog. It's so heavy most of the time, but I love it. I think it agrees with me. I've gained two or three pounds.

The rainy season has started. It's raining now, very softly—Gee! it makes me sleepy.

Buddy is fine. He is beginning to relax now. He can sit through the newsreel and it doesn't bother him so much. The doctor told him that's the best way to overcome that feeling. He loves shows, so that's where we spend most of our leisure time. He gets home on weekends and it surely is nice to have him home.

He is so wonderful to me. He does everything he can that he thinks will make my work easier. He's always bringing some little thing home for me.

Mom is sick, so that throws a little more responsibility on me. She was in the hospital for a week, but is home now. I don't know what is wrong with her. She spends everything they have on doctor bills. Poor Pa is so sweet about everything—does all the cooking and dish washing.

I'm sorry that Daddy hasn't been feeling well. I do hope he feels much better now. Give him and the others my love. I'll bet little Olivia is grown now. Oh! how I wish I could see her. As a matter of fact—I'd give anything to see all of you. I do hope that it won't be long before I can go home for awhile.

I'm glad that Henry and Thelma spent some time with you. I know Daddy was glad to see him. I'm so thankful that he came home in one piece.

Buddy and I took Betty out Saturday night. Oh! she's so sweet and I feel so sorry for her. I only pray that Charles will get to come home very soon.

I am still working and enjoying it. I have to make out my income tax return right away. They took out thirty-four dollars and I hope that covers everything.

Mother, I'm going to try to send some money next week when I get my bonus. I don't know yet how much I can send, but I'll do my best. I do want Doris' teeth looked after—soon. It will be quite expensive, but it's worth every penny it costs.

I do hope they get the pump in very soon. It will be much easier and much safer. I think about Olivia so much. I do hope she can't get too close to that well.

How are my little brothers? Give them my love and tell them to write me when they can. Kiss little Annette for me and tell her I'd like to hear from her, too.

Mother, I have to write a few letters for Mom now—so don't work too hard. Kiss everyone for me and write when you can.

>Lots & Lots of Love,
>Annelle

§

February 2, 1945

Friday

My Darling Mother,

I received your very sweet letter yesterday. It was so good to hear from you again. Your letters are almost like talking to you. Oh! I would give anything if only I could be there, talking to you—I think I have enough to talk about six months, without stopping!!! I only hope and pray that it won't be long before we can be together and just sit and talk.

Mother, I do hope all of you are feeling well. I think of you all the time. Please take care of yourself and don't work too hard.

I'm so glad that the material was satisfactory and the other things proved helpful. There was no belt to the slacks or the housecoat. Did you get the safety pins? I hope you did—I felt very lucky to find them.

Mother, you wanted to know if the material is plentiful out here. To be truthful—it is very hard to get. If Aunt Mattie wants some for house dresses, I can get all she wants. I have a good friend in the yardage and I can get it. It costs about 59 a yard. If she'll tell me how many dresses she wants and how much for each dress, I'll buy it for her.

"Mummy" we got in some nice house dresses. I'm putting a few in will call for you. I can't get them out for a week or so, but I'm paying on them now so you'll have them. I'm always getting Olivia some material for some dresses for I know that she outgrows hers so fast. I'm also going to get some cotton stockings to keep your feet and legs warm. It's just a few things, but it's something that's almost impossible to find out here and I think it may help you out. I would like to buy a nice outfit for everyone, but—you know—for some funny reason—they want money for everything—so consequently—I have to do as I can.

I had a letter from Buddy today. He is fine, but won't be able to come home this weekend. He asked me to send him money. He needed cigarettes and the little stinker plays cards at night—I can't say anything for that's about the only time he actually relaxes and to me that's worth a million dollars. He is beginning to be himself again. He is taking up commercial art and the instructor thinks he's terrific. His paintings are really marvelous. I'm very proud of him.

I'm not sure yet, but we may buy a house soon. We've been talking very seriously about it. I do hope we can. Oh! I'd be so happy. It has six rooms—it's not a big place, but nice. There are two bedrooms, a kitchen, living room, dining room, bath and den. Dave and Helen are buying one now and that encourages Buddy.

Gee! it's still raining. You can hardly get out. I could very easily use a yacht to sail around in. The rain doesn't help our business too much, either. We've hardly done anything for the last two days.

Tell Doris I appreciate her letter very much. I mailed Buddy's to him and I'm sure he'll be happy to hear from her.

"Mummy," please kiss everyone for me. Give them my love.
Write me all the news. I do love to get your letters.
I know you're tired of reading this letter so goodnight, "Mummy."

> *Lots & Lots of Love,*
> *Annelle*

§

February 13, 1945

Tuesday
Mother Darling,

I received two letters from you today and I was so glad to hear from you again. It was over two weeks since I heard and I was beginning to worry, especially since I heard there's a storm going on in Alabama.

I am happy that all of you are well except little Annett. Bless her heart. Tell her to please be careful.

Gee! you're sure turning out the quilts!! I'm sure glad you're able to quilt them for I know you need them. Out here we only have to have one blanket over us. The weather is never really cold. It's usually foggy, but not so cold.

I'm so sorry to hear about Noel. There are so many like him and many not so lucky, either. I'm glad that Earl was freed and I can only imagine how happy Mrs. Stutts is.

No Mother, Buddy doesn't play cards much. He doesn't go in for anything like that but when he's extra nervous, it relaxes him.

Mom's name is Sarah and Pa's is Abraham (Abe). They are both fairly well, but you know, they're getting old and can't do too much.

Well, I suppose we won't be buying a house. I think Dave is going into the army any time now. They're taking everyone—so he can't go on with his plans. Mannie may be getting married soon and we don't know what they'll do with Buddy—so we'll just have to wait.

Mother, I'm sending five dollars to help with Doris' teeth. It isn't much, but it's all I can do right now. I'll try my best to send more when I can.

I'm putting your dresses in Will Call tomorrow. I don't know when I can get them out.

Mother, take care of yourself and write often. Give my love to everyone.

> *Lots of Love,*
> *Your Sis, Annelle*

February 25, 1945

Sunday

My Dearest Mother,

I received your letter and the clippings yesterday. Thank you so much for both. I was so glad to hear from you again. You said it was a long time until you got my letter. I am sorry it was so long getting there!!!

I do hope all of you are well and not working too hard.

I'm glad you got the money all right. Mother, I was almost ashamed to send so little, but it was just the best I could do. I sent Buddy money because he hasn't been paid for over two months and he pays five dollars every week for fare and he buys all the cigarettes he can. Then—it costs quite a bit to live here—Twenty-two dollars just doesn't go very far.

Mom is in bed. She's been sick for a week. Mannie took her to a new doctor last Thursday and he put her on a diet. Pa is trying to do all the cooking and he isn't well, either. The doctor also put Mannie on a diet. Everyone in the house eats something different.

Buddy just left about two hours ago. He comes home on Friday night and goes back on Sunday. It is so terribly lonesome after he leaves. Mother, he asked me to tell you that he wanted very much to write to you, but he doesn't do any writing—He's so nervous. He sends his love to all of you. Bless his heart—if it isn't one thing to upset him, it's another. They're trying to get him to become an art instructor at the hospital and he doesn't want to because it would kill all his chances of getting out of the Army. Just being there—waiting—is very bad for him. He's been in the hospital for over six months. Oh! I pray that he will get out very soon.

Mother, Buddy and I looked everywhere for a kettle, brush and lamp top. They just aren't to be found. I'll keep looking when I can go into Los Angeles.

I'm sending a picture of Buddy and one that we had made last night. They aren't good, but the one of Buddy is so cute. He's making like my little boy.

We're having a fashion show next Thursday—I am going to model two play suits.

Oh! Gee! I'd give anything if only I could see all of you. It seems so long since I saw you. If only Buddy can get out and we can go to see you for a nice long visit.

Mother, kiss everyone for me and give them my love. Write as often as you can.

Yes, I wrote James Ed. but I suppose he hasn't had time to answer. How long has Charles Jr. been married? Carolyn looks rather cute! Nighty night Mother—

> *Lots & Lots of Love,*
> *Annelle*

§

March 5, 1945

Sunday

Mother Darling,

How is everyone at home? I do hope you are all well and not finding too much work to do.

Gee! it's raining here like anything—I think I'll be happy when the rainy season is over.

You know Mother, I thought I was happy that Saturday morning in November when I got Buddy's telegram that he was back in the states and then when he came home I was so terribly happy, but it's nothing compared to the happiness I experienced Friday afternoon, when soon after I got home from work, Buddy walked in—and told me that he was discharged. Oh! Mother it's so, so wonderful to see him in civilian clothes. We went into the men's department at the store Saturday and bought him some clothes—we got part of his wardrobe but he has to have a few more suits and more underwear—if we can find any. He looks so sweet in his new clothes. For a coming home gift—I gave him a beautiful cigarette lighter—it's pure sterling silver—handmade and I had it monogrammed. It costs twenty-two dollars and I let him pay for it—Nice, aren't I? Of course—he had the bank book—or at least what was once the bank book.

He won first prize at the art exhibit the day he left for the best painting. They gave him an oil paint set. Right now he's sitting beside me, making a painting for our bedroom. He's painting a face of an Arab.

Mom is still in bed, under the doctor's care. I hope this one can help her.

I got a letter from James Edward—He wrote a nice, long letter—I just answered it today.

I'm still working and I like it very much. It will be a few months before Buddy can work. The doctor's made him promise he would rest for two or three months. I suppose he'll go into radio or go to art school.

Mother, today I'm going to wrap a package for you—It's your house dresses and a few things I'm sending for Doris and some ties for Daddy.

That's about all the news—I'm still so excited about Buddy being out, I can hardly write. I wanted to send you a telegram, but Buddy wouldn't let me—he said he wouldn't because it might frighten you—so I'm writing.

Kiss everyone for me and give them my love. Buddy sends his love to everyone.

Lots & Lots of Love,
Annelle

§

March 9, 1945
[Written on S. H. Frees stationery]

Mother Darling,

Please forgive me for not having answered your letter sooner, but I've been going around in circles for the past few days. Nevertheless, I hope this finds all of you in the best of health.

I suppose you got my letter, telling you about Buddy being out of the army. Bless his heart—he's already started out, looking for work. I wanted him to rest for at least a month, but I soon found out that I could just as well be talking to the ocean—because he's just about that still. He is in the living room, working on an oil painting—he just stopped to make a few monkey faces. I just pray that he can get started in something—for he wants to so much.

Mother, thank you for sending Dan's letter. I want to write him. Would you please send me his address again. I misplaced the letter and I can't find it. It's hard to keep up with everything in one room.

Mom is much better, for which I am very thankful. She is up now and looks better. Pa is feeling better, too.

I saw in the news reel that it had been storming in Montgomery. I hope it doesn't get down to you.

I'll bet Olivia is growing like a weed. It seems funny to hear of all the things she can say because I remember her as a baby, just learning to run around. Oh! I'd give anything to see her.

Please thank little Annette for her very sweet letter. She sure is learning to write nicely.

Gosh! I'm so happy that Doris got braces on her teeth, after such a long time—I only wish I could help more. It costs quite a bit to buy Buddy's clothes because he needed everything—we only got two suits for him—I want to get him at least three more. We just can't find pajamas for him and shirts aren't so plentiful, either.

How are the boys? I'll bet they're as busy as little bees. Please give them my love. What is my Daddy doing these days? I know he's very busy. Give him my love and tell him to write when he can.

I know you are so very busy, Mother. I wish I could be there to help you. Maybe before too long we'll get to go.

There isn't much too much news, so I must close now. Write every time you can.

> Lots & Lots of Love,
> Annelle

P. S. Buddy sends his love to everyone and said he'd write as soon as he feels like it.

$

March 19, 1945

Monday
My Dearest Mother,

I received your letter today—also the one from Aunt Norma. I do hope all of you are well and not working too hard.

I'm glad you received the package and so glad the house dresses were all right. I was ashamed to send some of the things, but I couldn't get up courage to throw them out.

I was so glad to hear that Grandpa is better. I do hope all of you will be able to go to the birthday dinner.

Gee! Aunt Flora has a boy—that's wonderful. I hope he'll grow up to be as handsome as his Uncle Paul.

When you see Aunt Norma, Les and Jean, please give them our love. Also give our love to Jackie and family, Edna and baby, Virginia, Rex and Earl and Jernigan. I hope you get to see Uncle Terry and Uncle Max—Give them our love. Oh! Gosh!! I'd give anything to be there with everyone. If only!! Maybe before always!!

You asked if Rita Hayworth looks like her picture—well—no. Her complexion is not so good and her mouth isn't pretty, but she has beautiful hair. None of the stars except Donald O'Connor looks the same off screen. He's as cute as he is on screen.

We just heard Buddy's broadcast. Gee! he did a marvelous job—He will probably be home about eleven.

Mother, I'm rather tired today—we were quite busy so I must close so I can take a bath and roll my hair—I probably won't go to bed until Buddy comes home.

Please kiss everyone for me and give them mine and Buddy's love.

>*Lots & Lots of Love,*
>*Annelle*

P.S. Buddy is using the name Paul Frees for radio—He only has about twenty names.

§

March 23, 1945

Friday

My Dearest Mother,

I received your very welcome letter today and thank you so very much. I do enjoy your letters—It's just the next thing to talking to you and oh! how I wish I could do just that.

I know you must be very busy, especially what with trying to help Louise. I hope they're well by now. Say "hello" for me.

I'm glad you liked the dresses—we got in a few dresses today—There are three styles—I want to get you one of each. I'll put them in "will call" and when I can I'll send them. I'll put them away tomorrow because they are so hard to get—we've been waiting for them for over three weeks. They are inexpensive, but they'll be all right for house dresses. Aunt Minnie asked how much they are—well they're $3.95—I don't know if I have her size—Does she wear a twenty? If so, we have those.

I know little Olivia is a doll—I'd give anything to see her—I know she's grown so much. Please kiss her for me. Also give the others a kiss for me and give them mine and Buddy's love.

I'm so sorry that Daddy's throat has been sore—I do hope he feels all right now. Give him a kiss for me.

Gee! I'm so tired—last night Buddy and I went over to Davie's and they drove us out to San Fernando Valley to see a cousin—Davie goes into the Navy tomorrow—Gee! I hate to see him leave. We were up until 2:00—and the night before we were up until 1:30—Dave and Helen came over to say goodbye to Mom.

Mom and Pa are feeling all right now. Of course mom is blue with Davie leaving. You asked how old she is—She's fifty-nine.

Buddy sends his love and says he'll write when he isn't so nervous.

> Lots & Lots of Love,
> Your Annelle

§

March 30, 1945

Friday Night
My Dearest Mother,

I received yours and Annette's and Olivia's letters and as you know, I was so glad to get them. Oh! I could just see Olivia writing hers—It seems so funny though to hear about the things she talks about because when I last saw her, she was just learning to talk. Oh! what I would give to see her.

Buddy had to go to Hollywood tonight for rehearsals, so I decided I better answer your letter while I have the chance. He has to go tomorrow also—it being Saturday night—we'll leave from the store, go into Hollywood for dinner and then he'll go for rehearsals. He's on the *Lux Theatre* program Monday night. He's only going to do radio during his spare time. He starts to art school Monday and will go for four years. They pay him $103 a month, plus all expenses. Then, the few shows he can do, will help out. He was paid $75 for the first show he did and I suppose he'll get about the same for this.

We're trying to find an apartment, but it seems almost impossible. We want to save as much money as we can, so we can buy a house—someday. He goes to school 42 weeks a year—two and one half months for vacation—He's promised—the first vacation he gets, we're going to see you. Believe me, it can't be too soon. That's another reason we're trying to save money—to make the trip. It will cost us about $600.

He bought me a beautiful blouse today—when I got home—he had it hanging in the closet—it's a pink sheer, long sleeves, square neck with lace on the neck and sleeves. He doesn't know it yet, but I bought him a lovely robe in blue silk for Easter.

I put a deposit on your dresses and I want to get them out in a week or so, and I'll send them to you. There are three, not expensive, but all right for house dresses. I think I have a few more things to send also. I've gained about five pounds and I'm getting too fat for most of my clothes. I bought a suit about two weeks ago and now I can hardly wear it—where do I gain weight—on my "seat"—never my arms or shoulders.

I'll bet Annette looks adorable with her permanent. I'm so glad she got it.

Gosh! it doesn't seem as though Harold has been in the army long enough to have to go overseas. I do hope this will all be over very soon. Davis got in the navy—that's what he wanted.

Did they ever hear any more about James Reid? I hope that he is a prisoner and nothing happened to him.

Mom and Pa feel very well, but you know, they're getting old—

Please give Grandpa a big kiss for me and tell him I wish him many more happy birthdays. I'd sure like to be there.

I'm so sorry Daddy doesn't feel well. Give him my love and tell him I do hope he feels much better.

Kiss everyone for me and Buddy sends his love to everyone. He wants to go to see you.

Don't worry about me getting too close to the ocean—I never get a chance. I've never even been in the water.

No, I've never met Rita Hayworth—She comes in the store quite often. Buddy did a show for the army yesterday with Edward G. Robinson and he drove Buddy home.

Mother, that's almost all. I have a washing to do and last week's ironing, but I think I won't do it tonight. I'm rather tired. It was so hot today—I thought I'd die and you know how hot weather makes you feel.

Please take care of yourself and don't work too hard.

> Lots & Lots of Love,
> Annelle

P.S. You asked if we would have to make reservations a month ahead or plans? Yes—by plane or train—you have to have it a month in advance.

§

April 16, 1945

Monday
My Dearest Mother,
I received yours, Annette's and Olivia's letters and I was so very happy to get them. They were all so sweet.

I'm so glad you went to Grandpa's. Bless his heart—I'd sure like to see him. It must have meant everything to him to have all the children with him.

I do hope all of you are well and not working too hard. You must have plenty to do—without looking for it.

Everyone here is well. Buddy and I drove down to San Diego with Helen to see Davey—It was nice, but very tiring—It was the second Sunday we've driven down. We wanted to go down to Mexico, but in crossing the border, you must not have a "C" sticker on your car and we did.

I'm sure glad Willie D heard from James Reid and that he's safe. I only pray that they will all be home very soon.

Gee! I can hardly believe Aunt Jean is going to have another baby—Poor thing—I do hope this will be the last one.

Buddy did a show tonight—It was on the "Sherlock Holmes"—He did a terrific part—He's getting better all the time. He's still going to art school, but I think he's trying to do too much, but he can't keep still one minute so I suppose it's better he stays busy.

Please give my love to everyone and kiss each one for me. Buddy sends his love to everyone and says he thinks of you often and especially of the fried chicken!

I must say goodnight now—I'm so tired—Please answer when you can.

> Lots & Lots of Love,
> Annelle

§

April 28, 1945

Saturday

Dearest Mother,

I received your much appreciated letter yesterday—I was so happy to hear from you again. Your letters are almost like talking to you, but believe me I'd much rather be there talking to you in person.

I can't understand why it was almost two weeks until you heard from me. I've been writing as often as I did. I hope this letter won't be delayed.

If I make many mistakes just "chalk it up" to me being very tired. We had quite a hectic day at the store—we were very busy—Then the false report of the war being over—Everyone was so excited—and then I came home and cleaned my room and did a big ironing.

I am so sorry that poor Grandpa is still sick and can't see very well. Bless his heart as soon as I can I'm going to write him a letter. I had a letter from Aunt Les last week and I wrote her a nice long letter.

By all means eat plenty of chicken for Buddy and me. I'd sure like to be there to help eat about twenty pieces of it.

I only get a one week vacation—in August and I have to take it on my own time—Next year I get two weeks with pay.

Mom and Pa are fine—They're sitting on the couch, listening to the radio.

Buddy and I are on such a strict budget, we can't spend one penny for anything unnecessary.

I have to go to the dentist Tuesday to have my teeth cleaned—I hope he doesn't tell me I have any cavities.

Buddy is so tired—He's sleeping for awhile.

It sure seems good to know I can sleep late tomorrow.

Mother, please give everyone a big kiss for me and give them our love. I pray that it won't be forever before I can tell them myself.

Please forgive this short letter, but I am tired. Write me all the news.

I must close now.

> *Lots of Love & Kisses,*
> *your*
> *Annelle*

P. S. Did you get the package? Buddy says he will try to get time to paint a picture of me.

§

May 3, 1945

Thursday

My Dearest Little Sister,

I received your very lovely letter yesterday and I was so glad to get it. I should have answered last night, but I was rather tired. You will accept this, won't you, Darling?

How is everyone? I do hope they're well and thinking of me as I am of all of you.

Do you realize that it has been a year since I last saw you? Gee! it seems so, so long. I am only hoping that it won't be long before we can go. I'll bet I wouldn't even know you and the other for you must have grown quite a bit.

Buddy is working tonight. He goes to animation class every Thursday night.

I just cleaned my room and I have to wash when I finish this letter.

I do hope that you have received the things I sent by this time.

Darling, about you coming out here—I wish there was a way. But—First, there is no place for you to stay. Mom has a small apartment. She and Pa have a bed, Mannie is getting married and his wife will be here and Buddy and I have one bed. We just can't find an apartment. It's impossible—Second Darling, I don't have the money. It may sound funny to you, but it costs so much to live out here and Buddy and I are trying to save a little money to buy us a home. He goes to school and only gets $25 per week and I get $22 by the time they take out for income tax. It takes almost every penny for living expenses. The money he makes on the shows goes for his dues to the "Actor's Guild"—a club he has to belong to so he can work on the radio. I know you work to pay your expenses back, but until we can find a place of our own, it seems almost impossible. Please don't be angry, Darling. I'd give anything to have you with me, but that's the conditions.

It's been foggy here for the past week and rather cold tonight. I always have to wear a coat to work.

Please kiss Mother, Daddy, Joe, Jimmie, Annette and Olivia for me and give yourself a kiss.

I'm doing my own cooking now. We don't pay Mom anything for staying here now and she just isn't able to do all the cooking, so we cook for ourselves.

I wrote Grandpa a nice, long letter a few nights ago. Bless his heart, I do hope he feels better.

Darling, I must close now and do my washing. Please don't be mad with me for what I said. Be a good girl and write me a nice letter.

Give mine and Buddy's love to everyone.

> Lots & Lots of Love,
> Your Sis,
> Annelle

§

May 5, 1945

Saturday

Dearest Mother,

I received your letter yesterday and was more than glad to hear from you. I do hope everyone is well and not working so hard.

Buddy and I are fine and especially happy tonight. We just found an apartment today. I got it through one of the men at the store. It isn't such a beautiful place, but reasonable. Gosh! I'm so happy about it!! We looked everywhere for one, but until today was unable to find anything. We're moving tomorrow—I'm sure you don't envy us that task.

We ran around like crazy this afternoon, looking the place over and making arrangements.

We are fine and enjoying every minute. Buddy's doing very good in school. You should see some of his drawings. As soon as we get "set up" in our new place, he will make a picture of me for you.

Please kiss everyone for me and give them our love.

I'll write you a nice, long letter as soon as I can—until then, Goodnight Mother Dear. Let us hear from you.

> *Lots of Love,*
> *Buddy and Annelle*

P.S. The address is 1155—11th St. Apt. B. Santa Monica, Calif. Goodnight Mommy!

§

May 8, 1945

Tuesday

Dearest Mother,

I received your very sweet and much appreciated letter today. As usual, I was so happy to hear from you. I'm so sorry that you haven't heard from me in such a long time. As soon as I get "set up" here, I'll try to write more often. As you say, we've been so busy. It seems if I stop for one minute, I lose an hour in my work. Gee! I never knew there was so much work to keeping house. By the time I get home from work, shop for my groceries and make dinner, it's time to make lunches and go to bed. It won't be so bad when I catch up.

We went to Los Angeles yesterday and bought linens and towels. We also bought dishes and a radio.

Poor little Buddy is so tired—He's asleep on the couch now. He doesn't look too comfortable, so I'll have to wake him in a few minutes and get him to bed.

Isn't it wonderful about the war in Europe being over?!! It's almost too good to be true. May God bless all those boys and bring them to a complete victory over Japan very soon, so they can very soon rejoin their beloved wives and mothers.

I'm so happy for the Carroll's. I do hope Earl will recover all right. The Japs are so inhuman with our boys—Some will never overcome this sickness.

Gee! it must have been nice to have Miss Grant spend the day with you—and I'll bet she was interesting to talk to.

Mother, I wish just as much as you that we could be there with you on Mother's Day and eat fried chicken with you. Just keep saving it for us.

How is Grandpa? Bless his heart, I hope he's up and feeling much better.

Please kiss everyone for me and give them all our love. I'll bet all the children have grown so much, I couldn't recognize them. Tell them all to write me and when I can possibly find time, I'll answer. Let Olivia write me. Annette Darling, I haven't forgotten that I owe you a letter. Please forgive me, I've been so busy!! I'll get to it, though.

It's getting very late, Mother. Please forgive this writing.

Daddy, I know you are busy, but when you can, please write me a few lines.

I'll bet my little brothers are grown up now and have all the girls running after them. And my big sister, she must have plenty of boyfriends.

Please give them all mine and Buddy's love. I miss all of you so very much and I'm just waiting to see you. It seems like ten years.

I must go to sleep for I have to get up early.

Goodnight and lots & lots of love from your loving Son and Daughter—

Buddy and Annelle

P.S. "Mommy" please don't work so hard. You don't tell me, but I know you're running yourself from morning 'til night.

§

May 14, 1945

Monday

My Darling Mother,

After such a long delay, I'll try to write you about some of the things we've been doing during the past week.

First—Last Monday, we went into Los Angeles and bought a few things we needed for our apartment. We spent quite a hectic afternoon, trying to shop. There were so many people we could hardly walk. Tuesday I washed and Wednesday I ironed. Thursday Buddy worked until 10:00, so I did part of my cleaning and Friday I finished that and a few more pieces of clothes I had to iron. Saturday we were so busy at the store. I had $185.00 on my book and was I tired. Buddy doesn't go to school on Saturday, so he made dinner for me. We went to the show Saturday night and Sunday we went over to Mom's for a few minutes and saw Mannie and his fiancée. They're going to be married June 3rd.

Sunday night, Buddy had me pose for him about two hours. He's working on the painting now—It's an oil and it's good.

Mother Darling—I'm sending a card for Mother's Day and I'm going to send you something soon. I wanted to get it off last week, but I was so busy, I just couldn't find time. Believe it or not—it takes quite a bit of doing to work all day, cook, clean the apartment and find time to sleep! But I love it—It's really very much fun to have our apartment by ourselves.

Buddy still gets his head and stomach aches, but not quite so often. I hope in time, he will overcome them completely.

Please kiss everyone for me and give them mine and Buddy's love. Tell them all to write when they can. I know everyone is so busy and I think of you every minute.

Please don't work too hard and let us hear from you as often as possible.

Goodnight "Mommy" and lots & lots & lots of love,

Always your loving Son and Daughter,
Buddy and Annelle

§

June 4, 1945

Monday Night
My Darling Mother,

I received your very sweet and much appreciated letter this afternoon—oh! Gee! It's almost like talking to you. I can visualize everything you're doing and some things aren't so pleasant for I see you working so very hard. If only I could be there to relieve you for just one day.

This is also my difficult week and I didn't do my washing tonight as I should have, but there's always tomorrow and I'll feel better, so I'll do it then.

I know poor Daddy and the children are so busy. Please give them our love and tell them I think of them so often.

Little Olivia will be having a birthday—the day before Buddy's. Gee! I can't realize—She will be three years old. Bless her little heart—I'd give anything to see her. She's so precious.

My little Annette is such a sweet, smart little girl. I know that Christmas is a long way off, but I'm sure going to tell Santa Claus to be extra nice to her next time for she deserves it.

So—my big brother, Joe, is so strong, all he has to do is going breaking cultivators! That's a fine thing—I'll have to see if I can't get him something smaller to play with. Just kidding, Darling. And what about my Jimmie boy? How is he doing—I'll bet he's grown now and has more girls after him. My big sister is doing all right—Gee! she's grown up now and she's getting her teeth done nicely—She'll be so pretty, she would disown me if she could see me.

We went to Mannie's wedding yesterday and it was nice—very simple and lovely. He has a nice wife—She's isn't too beautiful and not too young—in her "thirties," but a lovely person. That was the first Jewish wedding I've seen and I thought it was very nice. The Rabbi called them under the canapé about four times before they finally started the ceremony. It was beginning to get funny. Dave and Buddy went to the reception, but Helen and I went to Helen's to feed Toni, then later went out to "Tropical Inn"—some little restaurant for chicken. Buddy ate and ate and ate—How he loves fried chicken.

Mother Darling, thank you so much for offering to send me some canned fruit, but I know you can use it and you work so hard to get it. I'll tell you something I'd like if you have it to spare, otherwise it's all right. That is, a small piece of bacon and a shoe stamp. Buddy needs shoes and he's already used all the stamps he has. I think I told you Phil Sherry is handling him for pictures and of course he has to have smart clothes when he goes in to see these producers. He has only two decent suits he can wear and I want him to have at least three or four more. Then he can buy one or two along until he has a nice wardrobe. Gee! but clothes are so terribly expensive out here. Gosh! you can easily spend two hundred dollars for one outright and have a fairly good looking suit.

I think Mannie and his bride (Eve) went to San Francisco for their honeymoon. Poor guy—I hope this one is for keeps.

We saw Betty a couple of weeks ago and she thinks Charles will be home before too long. Gee! I hope so. She's waited so faithfully for him. She deserves so much. Mary hears from Leslie regularly. Of course the poor kid is so very lonesome for him.

Say, about writing on the back of paper—I do it myself because it saves paper and I feel like I'm getting more when you use both sides and believe me, Mother, I enjoy your letters so very much.

I know poor Grandpa is getting old and I think about him so much. I was just talking about him to one of my girl friends tonight at dinner. She had dinner with me—Buddy is doing a show from 10:00—10:15 tonight. I suppose it will be quite late when he gets home. Bless his heart, he works so hard.

Mother, I'm going to send the portrait as soon as I possibly can. I'm ashamed I've waited so long to do it, but I've been busy.

Say, when you see Uncle Al, please ask him if he knows where he can buy some cigarettes. If he can send us some, Buddy will pay him well. Buddy brought home about twelve cartoons when he got out of the army, but they are gone and it's almost impossible to find any out here.

"Mummy" it's late now and I'm tired and I have a little headache, so I think I will have to make my lunch and go to bed.

Please give mine and Buddy's love to everyone.

> Lots & Lots of Love,
> Buddy and Annelle

P.S. Buddy's name is now: Paul Frees, so if you hear that name on the radio—that's him.

§

June 16, 1945

Saturday

My Dearest Mother,

I received your letter a few days ago and I was so happy to hear from you again. Honestly, I intended answering sooner, but I helped Buddy write some audition material the night I got your letter and yesterday I went to the blood bank and gave another pint of blood, but it didn't go so well with me this time and I had to take it easy. We've been so busy today and I'm exhausted—I had to come back to the Ladies' Lounge for a relief—so you see, it wasn't because I didn't want to.

I hope everyone is well! Gosh, Mother, I hate to think of you getting up so early and doing all that canning plus your other work. I only wish I could be there to help you. Even if I'm not, you can be sure I think of you every minute.

Mother, it's sweet of you to offer to send ham and believe me we would appreciate it—you can't buy it for love nor money out here. It's quite all right about the shoe stamp, Mother—I got some non-rationed shoes. No, I don't have Jimmie's no. 3 book—if I did, I'd send it to you.

You said Uncle Al had retired. Do you think he would sell Buddy his typewriter? Buddy needs one, but so far has been unable to find one.

I hope you have received the portrait by now—It's a beautiful picture, but it doesn't look like me too much.

Buddy's birthday is next Friday. I'm giving a surprise party for him and I'm making the cake myself. Gee! I hope it comes out good. I'm only inviting Betty and a girl friend Jeanne Beck—Our place is so small and too it's on the second floor and we can't have so much noise. I'm giving him a gabardine coat and a portable bar—I hope he likes them.

Tomorrow's Father's Day and I wish I could send Daddy something—even a Buick or something—but—maybe when Buddy gets into pictures.

He hasn't gotten anything yet, but of course it takes time. Phil thinks he will be a star—I hope so. It sounds funny, but Phil, Buddy's agent, laughed at a man that wanted to buy one of his clients for $1,000 per week—so you can get an idea as to money that's involved—just in case he gets anything!!!

I tried to do my ironing, but my clothes had soured so I had to wash them out again.

I suppose we will go over to Mom's tomorrow—I think Mannie and Eve will be there.

Did I tell you Buddy bought me a new suit, dress, two hats, a bag, three prs. shoes and a pr. of earrings. I needed them, too, but he needs clothes even worse.

Have you heard from Grandpa lately? I do hope he's feeling good. When you write him, give him our love.

Gosh! I'll bet all the children have grown so much and I'd give anything to see them and my little Olivia—Kiss her for me and thank her for her kiss—Please kiss everyone and give them our love.

Please write me all the news and don't work so hard!

> Lots & Lots of Love,
> Your daughter and Son,
> Buddy & Annelle

§

June 21, 1945

Thursday

My Dearest Mother,

I received your very sweet letter two days ago and I was so happy to hear from you again. Please forgive me for not having answered before now, but Gee! I've been so busy preparing for Buddy's birthday party I'm giving him Saturday night. It's a surprise and I have quite a bit of undercover work so he doesn't know. I've worked my legs off, trying to find chicken and no one has any. I think I may get two rabbits tomorrow—I hope so.

He is going over to Catalina Island to do a show Friday and will get back Saturday just in time for the party.

I've done my washing and ironing for this week and took all my slip covers off and curtains down and washed and ironed them. I'll do my cleaning tonight and make his cake tomorrow night.

Gosh! it's been raining here all day, but looks as though the sun may come out later.

Well, I didn't get to finish this at work, so I'll start again.

It's after ten—we just got back from Mom's. She gave me ten eggs—That's something else that's hard to get. Everything's hard to get out here.

Actually there's no news. I'm still working and it seems I'll never catch up with all my housework—It's a probem with two full-time jobs.

Today is little Olivia's birthday and I thought of her, but I just couldn't get around to sending anything. Perhaps someday I'll get around to getting all the gifts I'm supposed to.

This is such a short letter—but please forgive me. I'm tired and it's late. Buddy is sleeping already—Just let that guy look at a bed and he starts snoring.

Please give everyone our love and a big kiss, too. For yourself—three kisses each.

> *Goodnight, Mommy,*
> *Lots & Lots of Love,*
> *Your Buddy & Annelle*

§

June 29, 1945

Friday

My Dearest Mother,

Please forgive me for not having answered your letter before now, but honestly—I've been so terribly busy. I worked all last week preparing for the party and this week, I've been cleaning up after it.

Everything turned out perfect. I made the cake, but my frosting was too soft, so I bought one and put the candles on. I had everything all set when he came home that night and everyone was here—Gee! was he surprised—and happy. We were up until after two in the morning. Betty and Jeanne Beck stayed overnight. I gave him the coat (it was too small so he took it back and got a suit). Then I gave him the portable bar—Mom gave him $25.00, Betty gave him aftershave lotion, Mannie and Eve a carton of cigarettes and Jeannie gave him a beautiful card. He was so very happy and so was I because he was.

Buddy asked me to tell you that he appreciated your letter so very much and would write as soon as he could. Bless his heart, he's so busy these days. He goes to school every day and almost every night he has a rehearsal and gets home about midnight. He also has about three auditions a week and has to go to the different studios with Phil to try for pictures.

We're fine and very happy, but quite busy all the time. I'm working every day and at night I either wash or iron or clean but I love it and you too.

Jeanne is here and another girl friend Gabrielle Pritchard, an artist's daughter—Buddy's rehearsing.

How's little Olivia and the others? Please kiss them all for me. I'd give anything if I could only see all of you. Maybe before always.

Do you ever see Frances and Aunt Minnie, Aunt Ollie and Aunt Mattie? Give them my love. How is Grandpa? Bless his heart, I do hope he is feeling well again. What about Aunt Norma and Aunt Les? Do you hear anything from Aunt Jean, Edna or Katherine? I'd sure like to know how they are. Give them our love.

Mother, would you please ask Uncle Al would he like to sell his typewriter? I'd like to buy it for an anniversary gift for Buddy with a nice desk.

I haven't heard from Mary Lou for so long—I'm worried about her—I wish I'd get a letter.

Gee! the weather is funny out here. I'd like to see summer for a change.

"Mummy" that's about all the news. Please write me all the news about everyone. I must say goodnight now. Please don't work too hard and let me hear from you.

Kiss everyone for me and give them our love.

Goodnight "Mummy" and sweet dreams.

> *Lots and Lots of Love,*
> *your loving son and Daughter,*
> *Buddy and Annelle*

§

July 1, 1945

Sunday
Dearest Mother,

I received your letter yesterday and was I happy to hear from you. That was the nicest one I've gotten in a long time—It sure made me feel good.

I hope everyone is feeling good and having a nice rest today. I think I could have slept this day through, I was so sleepy.

Buddy just left to do a show tonight, so he had to go for rehearsal this afternoon. Gosh! I hardly see him. He does about two shows a week and will do one a week on Catalina Island. He's also rehearsing every night for a stage play to be presented in a month or so—He's still going to art school and Phil keeps taking him to all these different studios. I don't know what will happen as far as pictures are concerned—It takes so long to get lined up.

I was surprised to hear about Aunt Jean's new baby—I thought I had dreamed you told me that she was expecting one. I hope she gets along all right.

Gee! I was happy to hear that Dan is in Oakland—I sure wish he would come to see us on his furlough. When you write him, give him our address and tell him where I work—so he can come down. I am on the second floor in Sportswear at Henshey's in Santa Monica. Gee! I'd like for him to come over for a few days.

When Uncle Al knows how much he wants for his typewriter, let me know— If he doesn't want too much, I'll buy it.

I just wrote Mary Fussell a letter. I'm worried about her—it's been so long since I heard from her.

Gee! why! I have to take a shower and then I think I'll go to sleep for awhile. I thought I'd go see Donald O'Connor's latest picture, but I think I'd rather sleep. I think they sent Don overseas—Poor kid, he's so weak looking, a strong wind would blow him away—I don't know what they'll do with him over there, he doesn't entertain the boys.

Mother, I wrote you a letter Thursday so there really isn't much news—so I must close now.

Please kiss everyone for us and give them our love.

Thank you so much for sending the ham and I'm sure it will be good—Don't worry about getting the jam and stuff off. We can use it anytime.

I will write again when I get a chance.

Bye—Bye "Mummy."

Lots & Lots & Lots of Love,
Your loving Son & daughter,
Buddy & Annelle

§

July 4, 1945

Wednesday

My Dearest Mother,

I received your very sweet letter Monday and was so happy to get it. I wanted to answer it sooner, but I was so busy I just couldn't get to it.

I do hope everyone is feeling well and enjoyed today. I only hope before the next fourth of July we shall have conquered the Japanese and can celebrate freely.

Buddy did a show last night and then rehearsed until eleven. I had dinner with a girl friend, Lois Keen (Her father was once governor of Guam)—so Buddy came over and we stayed overnight. I haven't felt so good today—I've been in bed—Nothing unusual, just my usual sickness. Dr. Pearson is going to start giving me shots next week so I won't have any pain. He gave Buddy some codeine pills for me to take this time.

You probably can't read this. I'm lying in bed while I'm writing and my hands are so weak. It's because I gave blood to the Red Cross three weeks ago and I haven't had time to build it up yet.

Poor little Buddy has been so busy today—we came home about twelve and then he walked five blocks to the market and while he was there, he called the doctor and then had the prescription filled and came home and made lunch, did the dishes and cleaned everything. Then he made dinner and cleaned the kitchen and he timed the pills I took and repeated them when it was time. Gosh! the one day I had off and I had to spend it in bed.

Mother, we received the ham and thank you so very much—as much as I hate to say it—I'm afraid we had to throw it out—It had worms in it. It's such a long trip and I suppose it was quite hot coming out here. Thank you so much for your thoughtfulness anyway.

How is everyone? I do hope the children are fine. Bless their hearts. I wish I could see them. I dreamed of Doris last night. I thought I had two watches and she gave one of them away. I wanted her to have it, but she wouldn't keep it.

If Aunt Minnie wants any materials, I'll get it for her. She'll have to tell me how much she wants. It's about sixty-nine a yard. They don't send anything out of town C.O.D., but I'll pay for it and she can pay me. They only give four yards per customers of each piece of material. It's very hard to get. I have the lady put it away for me. I just bought some beautiful gingham for table clothes. I want to get some for dresses to make for the girls. I don't know when it will be for they don't always have it.

How is Daddy? I do hope he and Joe aren't working so hard. I think they're doing wonderful. I'm so happy for them.

Mother, I'm rather tired, so I must close now. Please don't work too hard and let me hear from you as often as you have time to write.

Please give our love to everyone.

Goodnight "Mummy."

> *Lots & Lots of Love,*
> *your loving son & daughter,*
> *Buddy & Annelle*

§

July 10, 1945

Tuesday

My Dearest Mother,

I received your very sweet letter yesterday and was of course so glad to hear from you again. I would have answered last night, but Mom came over and had dinner with me and wanted me to answer a letter to Rose. Jeanne was here also—so with everything I just didn't get to it. You asked me if Jeanne is in pictures—No, she isn't but she should be. She is a beautiful girl—She used to work here.

I am so sorry that Aunt Norma is sick. Poor Aunt Les—I know she must have her hands full. I've thought of them so much. I hope Aunt Norma is feeling much better by now.

Gee! it's beautiful here today. I didn't even have to wear a sweater to work and you can know by that—it's summer in California.

I started this last night after I got into bed—about midnight and I had no more than started when Buddy came home and he was so very tired I turned out the lights so he could go to sleep. He's been working so very hard lately—day and night! He doesn't have to rehearse anymore this week, so maybe he can get some rest.

I am going to the doctor Saturday to have a wart taken off my finger and I have to go next week to another doctor to take some shots for my monthly sickness. He thinks he can help me. I hope so. Gee! it seems everything comes up at once. I have to get something for Buddy for our anniversary and I just don't know what it will be. I'd like to buy a desk for him, but the only one I saw that I liked was $109.50 and I just can't pay that much.

Well—here I am again—I started writing this again when I got to work and didn't get to write much before the bell rang so after I finished my lunch, thought I'd begin again. It's almost time to go back.

I hope my big brother is feeling well again. He and Daddy are sure doing well. I hope they can keep it up. How are the others? Please give all of them our love and a big kiss. I'll bet little Olivia is quite grown up now.

Mother, this is really getting to be a joke—I started this night before last and I'm still writing. I just can't seem to get enough time to finish it.

Anyway—I was so happy to know that Aunt Jean is feeling all right. I like the baby's name. Is he as sweet as Earl? Do you ever hear anything from Edna and her baby—and Katherine and her family? I'd sure like to see them or at least hear from them. Oh! about Aunt Flora and her baby! Have you seen him? I'll bet he's a darling.

I got a letter from Frances and she asked to send her a couple of house dresses. I can't send them C.O.D. and I just don't have the money right now. I want to send them as soon as I can. I will send Doris a dress as soon as I can, also. I wish I could now, but I just can't. We're trying to save money and too everything is so expensive. Buddy isn't set up yet. It takes a long time and it cost quite a bit for him to pay club dues and have "cuts" made of his programs and a million other things so all in all it's taking about all we make to keep up with everything.

Mother, it's almost time for the bell, so I must close now because I have so much work to do.

Please kiss everyone and give them our love. Buddy will write as soon as he can find time.

> Lots & Lots of Love,
> Your loving Son & daughter,
> Buddy & Annelle

§

July 13, 1945

Friday

My Dearest Mother,

I received your's and Annette's very sweet letters last night and I don't have to tell you how happy I am to get them. Gee! it makes me feel good after reading your letters. I just finished answering the letter I got from you Monday and honestly, I'm ashamed that it took me so long to finish it, but I find so much to do every night that by the time I've done my work it's time to take my shower and go to bed.

Buddy didn't have to rehearse last night, but did his regular program and got home about 9:30—so as soon as he came in, I made something for him to eat and then we went to sleep early for the first time in over a month. It sure was good, too because I hadn't had any sleep worthwhile for a long time.

Thank you Annette Darling for the sweet little letter you wrote. I wish you would write more often. I think you're quite a little lady to take Olivia to stay overnight with Aunt Mattie. I'll bet you were such a good little Mother that she just didn't think of crying. Please give her a big kiss for me and give the others one for me, too. Now—can't you do that for Sis? Thank you Darling!!

The bell just rang, so I'll have to finish this later—O.K.?!!

Well, here I am again—I just had my lunch and decided I should get started again.

I was just telling one of the girls all about my family—How close we are to one another and the names and ages. She thought it was wonderful to have such a nice family—But she just couldn't know until she's seen you!

Gee! "Mummy" I miss all of you so much—Honestly, no one knows. I sure wish I could go back for even a day—I think I'm going Christmas—I know I am if it's at all possible.

Well, it seems as though this letter is going to turn out like the other—I started it last night and I'm still writing. I suppose it isn't a bad idea after all though—because I got the letter you wrote July 9th, today, so I'll just answer it while I'm writing.

Gee! it seems so good when I come by the box at night after a long day's work and find one of your letters there. It relaxes me so to read them. I think you do a better job every time—at least I seem to enjoy each one more.

Well "Mummy," you don't have to worry about me going to the blood bank anymore. Buddy gave me my orders the day they brought me home from them. It frightened him so much.

I feel very good tonight. We had a big day at the store—but I came home, went to the market and got the things I needed, then I made my dinner and ate very slowly—completely relaxed. Then I did the dishes and took a good shower, rubbed myself with oil and combed my hair and put on a playsuit! Gee! it's nice, too!! It's rather warm here and I have all the windows open. There is a breeze coming through—I'm sitting in the middle of the bed, enjoying myself. Mother, you know I feel almost as if I'm talking to you—and oh! how I wish I was.

Please Darling, we didn't expect you to send Buddy anything for his birthday—just knowing that you thought of him made us happy.

About the typewriter now—I know Uncle Al has taken very good care of it and I know it's a good one because I've used it, but I'm afraid he's asking too much—It just isn't worth that much. By the time we got it shipped out here, it would cost another five or ten dollars—so just tell him we appreciate it, but we decided we couldn't buy it. By the way, you didn't tell me in the last letter how much he wanted, so it's good you wrote me in this one.

"Mummy" Darling, please don't worry about the ham. I know it was in perfect condition when it left you, but it's to be expected that it wouldn't keep until it got here because it's very hot. Now you be a good "Mummy" and don't worry about it. It was very sweet of you to go to the trouble of sending it. Please don't worry about sending the jam for you have enough to think of as it is. When you send it, we can use it, so anytime is good.

Buddy did his regular show tonight so he won't be in for another thirty or forty minutes.

Poor Daddy and Joe—I know they're working so hard and I think about them as well as the rest of you all the time. Please tell Daddy to write me—just a few lines when he can and feels like it.

Mother, I know that you are kept busy, every minute and believe me, I think of you. I just wish I could be there with you and help with some of your work.

I've been rather busy for the past few weeks—I haven't been out in so long—I probably couldn't know how to act.

"Mummy," I could go on like this for many more pages, but you must be very tired of reading this, so I'll save the rest for next time.

Buddy sends his love to everyone. Please kiss all for me.

> *Lots & Lots of Love,*
> *your loving son & daughter,*
> *Buddy & Annelle*

§

July 26, 1945

Thursday
My Dearest Mother,

I received your very sweet letters a few days ago, and I'm very sorry that I haven't answered before but honestly you should see the way I've been running around the past week.

111

I hope you're feeling good "Mummy." I think of you all the time and wish that I could be there with you. Buddy and I had already started planning on going home to see you when he gets his vacation—so naturally something had to happen. I hope go to the hospital in a few weeks. It's nothing serious. Just a small tumor to be removed. I have a very good doctor—so there's nothing to worry about. The only thing I'm worried about is the money—It takes just about twice as much as we have saved. Always something. Just as we think we'll really start saving, something always comes up.

A few days ago Buddy went to Hollywood and bought a car—a '40 Chevrolet. He went to the ration board and got an "A" and "C" book and went back to the place to bring the car home and surprise me—so the first thing he did before he got out of the lot, he ran into a car and bent our car up. His nerves went to pieces so he had to take it back and now he has to pay about seventy-five dollars for damages. If anything else happens—!!!

Doris Darling—I have the dress for you and will send it as soon as I possibly can. I also had a little hat I'm going to send for you to wear with it. Buddy thinks the dress will be beautiful on you and was so interested in picking the right one. We wanted to get something else for you, but just couldn't after everything turned out as it has. I want to get it over with so we can hurry and get it paid for. I will only lose about three weeks so it isn't too bad. I also have insurance to cover part of it.

How is my Darling little Olivia and Annette? Gee! how I wish I could see them. There was a little girl in the store the other day and she sure looked like Annette. It made me so homesick to see her.

I hope this letter doesn't turn out like the last one I started so many times. I started this one this morning and just finished my lunch, so decided I'd try to finish it.

Other than what I've told you, everything is about the same. Mom is in the Glendale Sanitarium—just resting.

My wort is fine. It didn't bother me at all. He burned it out.

If you don't hear from me for awhile—I'll let you know about everything. Please don't worry.

"Mummy" I just can't think of anything else so I suppose I'll have to close now. I'll write again as soon as I can.

Please kiss everyone for me and give them our love.

Lots & Lots of Love,
Annelle

§

July 31, 1945

Dearest Mother and All;

I wrote a letter in answer to your last one a few days ago, but have been carrying it around in my bag and kept forgetting to mail it. I've had so much on my mind these past few days. I received the letters from Doris, Jimmie and Annette and just decided to make this a big one. I do hope everyone is feeling well. I know you are very busy and I think about all of you.

I went to another doctor since I wrote the last letter. He is just out of the army and is a female specialist—His name is Koennecke and is supposed to be very good. He gave me a more thorough examination and found about the same as Dr. Mahoney. He also said that my blood was very low and he would have to build me up before the operation. I'm taking some iron capsules and little white tables. I think I'll go to the hospital in about three weeks. He is much more reasonable than the other doctor. We won't have to go in debt this way, but it will take all we have and Buddy won't let me talk about going back to work within six weeks. I do have the insurance that will help quite a bit, though.

We went to San Fernando Valley yesterday and it was beautiful out there—we spent the afternoon and evening with Buddy's agent, Phil Shelly. They are lovely people. Buddy is quite busy—just keeps going all the time. Bless his heart, he never gets any rest—but never complains.

We celebrate our 2nd anniversary tomorrow. It's our first together and I think he has to work. Oh! well—such is life.

I must thank my darling little sisters and brother for their lovely letters—I appreciate them more than you can ever know. Let's have more of them.

What happened to Dan's furlough? I never heard anything from him. I thought he would spend a few days with us, but I never heard from him.

Mother—I must say goodbye now—I thought I had so much to say, but I suppose I don't.

Jimmie Darling—your art is very good. You'll have to come out and draw with Buddy.

> *Lots of Love,*
> *your Annelle*

§

August 4, 1945

Saturday

My Dearest Mother,

I hope everyone is well. I didn't get a letter this week, but maybe that's because I didn't get my letter off to you sooner.

There isn't anything new. We celebrated our second anniversary Wednesday night. Jeanne Beck and Lois Keen had dinner with us. Lois gave us a glass top coffee table which is very lovely. Jeanne is making chair covers and table-cloths to match—She didn't get it finished in time. I gave Buddy a shirt and four pairs of socks and he bought a typewriter for us. We couldn't afford to give anything expensive.

I still haven't sent Doris' dress and I'm ashamed of myself. Maybe I will get it off Monday. It's hanging in my closet, just waiting for me to send it.

This is my unlucky day. I went to work this morning, but one of the girls had to bring me home. I feel better now, but I'm still in bed.

Buddy went fishing today—He went out on a small boat with a friend of ours and he caught two fishes. Gee! was he excited—I haven't seen him happier in ages. He needs more sun and relaxation. He sure got burned, but good.

We were going out to the Valley tonight, but I had to be sick.

Betty is coming over tomorrow and I can hardly wait to see her. She's so nice and sweet. We think Charles is coming home in September and I pray that he will. I will be so happy for them.

We got a letter from Davey this week and he flunked out on Radar. It's a very stiff course and they pass only about eight or ten percent of all that go—So I suppose Davey will have to go to sea as soon as they have assigned him to a ship. He and Helen had their fifth anniversary today. Poor kids—him in Chicago and her out here.

There hasn't been such beautiful weather since I've been here. It's really nice.

I called Dr. Koennecke today and he hasn't been able to get a room for me yet, but he will know Monday when he can get one, so I don't know when I'll have my operation. I will be very happy when it's all over. I'm not afraid, but I want to feel good for a change.

I haven't heard from Mary Bankert in such a long time. I'm sure worried about her. I pray that nothing is wrong.

Do you hear from Aunt Les, Aunt Norma and Grandpa? I hope everything is well with them. What about Aunt Jean and her family. If Edna, Kathy and

Virginia don't have my address, please give it to them and tell them to write us! It would be a very pleasant surprise to get a letter from my cousins. How is Frances—and her baby? Is Harold still at Fort Benning? I hope so. Please give our love to Aunt Minnie, Aunt Mattie, Aunt Ollie, Uncle Al, Betty, Frances, Aunt Kathleen, Uncle Charles, Laura, Uncle Gene, Uncle Charlie and the others. I'd still like a picture of Aunt Flora's little Charles—I'll bet he's a darling. It's still hard to imagine her a mother.

Now—how are my darling little sisters Olivia, Annette and Doris? I know they aren't "little" anymore, but to me they will always be! And how are my big brothers? I know better than to call them little brothers? Last but by no means least—how are you and Daddy? I know that both of you are so busy and have so many responsibilities. I think of you all the time and wish so much that I could be there, but—!!

I'm getting tired "Mummy" and a little weak, so I must say goodnight now. Please let me hear from you as often as you possibly can—I understand though when I don't hear.

Buddy sends his love to everyone and says he is going to surprise you with a letter before long.

Lots & Lots of Love from both
    Your loving Son & Daughter,
    Buddy & Annelle

§

August 9, 1945
[First typewritten letter]

Dearest Mother,

I received your letter and as you know, I was so very happy to hear from you again. Your letters are always so interesting and I enjoy them so much. I do hope that everyone is well and not working so hard.

Mother please don't worry about me. As I told you before there is nothing to worry about. I'm sure that I will be all right. There isn't anything serious about the operation and it will only be a short time and I will be home, resting and taking it easy, which is the really important thing. I go to the hospital on the 21st and have the operation the next day. Helen will be there with Buddy while they do the operation and I will feel much better. We were over at her house last Saturday night and she gave me a beautiful bed jacket. I bought one and two nightgowns to use while I'm there. I have to get a few more.

Gee; I can hardly believe that Joe is six feet tall and Jimmie is so grown up. It seems only yesterday that they were only babies, but you just can't keep up with them. You said that Olivia was a tall and slender little girl. I can hardly believe that, either. I still see her as a little girl that is almost as round as she is tall. They all must have grown so much. I only wish that I could see them. I miss everyone so much and just live for the time when I go for a visit, but if I keep having to have operations, we won't have any money for anything.

I finally got a letter from Mary and I was very thankful to get it, too. Les came back from overseas and is stationed in Oklahoma for eight weeks and then if the war isn't over he will have to go to the Pacific. I only pray that it will be over before then. From the looks of things it will be over any time now. If it isn't, I am very [sorry] for the silly Japs because they will get it but good and I don't care if they do because they deserve anything we give them. The Atomic bombs we have aren't anything to play with, but it seems that they will have to find out the hard way. They have been stalling long enough and I think it is time to wake them up with a few of our new invention. Gee; but everyone was excited when that false report came in last night and they had a right to be. We were eating dinner in a delicatessen in Ocean Park when the word came in and I was so excited I could hardly eat.

Mannie and his wife Eve came over to our house last night and stayed awhile with us. They seemed to think that our apartment was very nice. I don't see anything so nice about it, but it will be all right [when] we can get a place of our own.

Well, I hope that I get some mail from my cousins and aunts very soon now that you are going to give them my address. Now they will have no excuse. I know that Aunt Flora's baby is a darling and I wish that I could see him.

Gosh; I get so tired all the time. I can't do anything without getting so tired I can hardly see. I will be glad when I'm out of the hospital and then I will feel much better.

The girl that Louise told you about didn't make me feel too happy, but I'm sure that nothing like that is wrong with me and I'm really not worried.

Please give our love to everyone and tell them I would give anything to see them. Buddy would write as I said before but bless his heart he is always working. Tonight he is rehearsing for the play. He hasn't been feeling too good for the past few days. His stomach is bothering him and he doesn't feel like doing anything but resting and relaxing when he is home. Talking about the fish he caught, he went fishing the other day and brought back seven bass that weighed about a pound each. He thought that the two of us could eat them for dinner. We finally gave them to our neighbors and they were very happy to get them.

I sure didn't like to clean them and I told him he could just leave them at the boat next time.

Mummy, I'm tired now so I think will have to close. Thank you again for the very nice letter that you wrote this week. I do enjoy them.

I do think Daddy and the others are very smart to have picked a bale of cotton already and had it ginned. I hope you make a good crop this [time] and get plenty to tide you over very nicely.

Little Jeanne Beck, the one that you thought was an actress, is here and she sends her best regards to you and the others.

You wanted to know about how Buddy is getting along with pictures. Well, he has to lose a bit of weight before he can get into pictures so he is going to take reducing pills so his face will get thinner. Phil still takes him to the different studios and is doing everything for him that he can and I don't think it will be too long before he will get something but he is quite busy with this play he is doing but after that I'm sure that he will get something.

Goodnight Mummy…please don't work hard and let me hear from you.

Lots and lots of love…Your Buddy and Annelle

§

August 16, 1945
[Last letter; second typed letter]

Dearest Little Sister,

I received your very sweet letter the other day and of course I was very happy to hear from you after such a long time. I know that you are very busy and I understand. I do hope that you are well and not working too hard.

Isn't it wonderful about V J Day? I was so happy when we heard the news over the radio that I cried and laughed at the same time. Everyone was in a dither and the customers were the same way. We closed the store a few minutes after we heard the news. No one could do anything. I went over to a girl friend's house and had dinner with her as Buddy wasn't home at the time. When we went out into the streets, everyone was throwing pennies and paper all over the streets and throwing anything else that they could find to throw. They started shooting firecrackers and a few other things. Bells were ringing and people were talking, laughing and crying. No one was hearing what the other was saying. We can sure say that we lived in the [most] historic time of all the world. What with the new Atomic bomb and everything else. If only we can keep our noses out of everybody's business but our own now, we will be all right. I just pray that this will be lasting peace. We celebrated that night. A couple of our friends came over in their car and took us out to the Valley to see Phil and his family. They were celebrating, too. We stayed until two in the morning. Oh, but it is wonderful. I can hardly believe it. Now the boys will come home to their wives, babies and sweethearts. The ones that have never seen their babies will be so happy to be home for keeps. God bless all of them for what they have [been] through and done and may they live in peace.

I am not working now. I quit Tuesday and will not go back until after my operation.

Buddy just left for rehearsal and he will be gone until about midnight so I think I will go over to Mom's and stay for awhile.

Darling, at last I am sending your dress and hat. I am also enclosing a belt that belongs to a dress that I sent you a long time ago. I can't send the package until tomorrow because the post office is closed today, but I will surely get it off then. Please forgive me for waiting so long to send it but I have had so much on my mind that I just couldn't think of it. I will see what I can do about selecting your school clothes for you but I won't be at the store for a couple of months so I will have to wait and see what happens.

Please give little Olivia a big kiss for me and tell everyone hello for us and that we would like very much to see them. Maybe someday in the not too distant future, we will be able to go home for a nice, long visit. Would you like that?

Gee, they sure got some of the things off ration lists fast. Gas and all canned goods. Buddy and I went shopping this morning and it was really a pleasure because we didn't have to fool with ration stamps except for meat.

The weather is so beautiful out here. Maybe it was just waiting for the war to be over. Anyway, it is nice.

Honey, I must say goodbye for now because I have to get dressed to go to Mom's and I want to get there before too late. Be a good girl and help Mother so she won't have so much to do.

Bye Bye and remember that I love all of you and miss you so much. Give everyone a big kiss for us and save one for yourself.

LOTS AND LOTS OF LOVE,
YOUR SISTER AND BROTHER,
ANNELLE AND BUDDY

§

www.ingramcontent.com/pod-product-compliance
Lightning Source LLC
Chambersburg PA
CBHW051839020726
47502CB00005B/1870